OUT OF EGYPT

M. ELIZABETH CROUSE

ILLUSTRATED BY PHOTOGRAPHS

ISBN: 978-1-63923-707-4

All Rights reserved. No part of this book maybe reproduced without written permission from the publishers, except by a reviewer who may quote brief passages in a review to be printed in a newspaper or magazine.

Printed: February 2023

Published and Distributed By:
Lushena Books
607 Country Club Drive, Unit E
Bensenville, IL 60106
www.lushenabks.com

ISBN: 978-1-63923-707-4

A NUBIAN VENDOR OF TRINKETS

TO
MY FRIEND

INTRODUCTION

ONE morning in Cairo the author was talking with a young American collector. "When you know Egypt," he said, proudly handling a beautiful little figure of Osiris, "you cease to believe anything. You find that thousands of years ago, the Egyptians had in their religion all the things which you believed!"

Others, who know Egypt more superficially, frequently make similar remarks. But, as the collector spoke, a strong feeling came to the author that the discovery of these religious ideas in Egypt, should not give a denial, but rather a confirmation to our own belief.

So she set herself seriously to study what the explorers and the historians have to tell. That she has expressed in this volume what she found is due to the need of which she became conscious in her studies; the need for something to express Egypt as a whole.

Therefore: This book is neither a guide book nor a history, but a series of essays combining the descriptions incident to the Nile journey, with historical sequence and religious significance, in an endeavor to progressively reveal the development of Egypt and its place in the development of the world. The excellent guide-books, while giving many details, are necessarily fragmentary, and assume a background of connected knowledge which they require for full intelligibility. On the other hand, of large and technical books there is no end. Whole histories and studies of special periods or phases, these are the great store-houses of the knowledge of the Past, the gift to the Present of men, who, through prodigious and untiring labor and life-long devotion have opened up the earth and unsealed the inscriptions, permitting us to enter the mystic world that was before us. A sight of the "treasures of darkness" awakens the wonder of that labor, and makes the writer, whom these wise men have admitted to that Past, but who has not held a spade or a cipher, very humble in offering her guidance to others. Yet few readers or travellers have time to learn for themselves all that the savants have produced—the interpretation of which changes so rapidly, that the knowledge of twenty-five years ago is completely revised, and in some cases, reversed. A book based upon the recent findings, which should combine description with history and religious interpretation, might, by revealing Egypt, as an articulate whole, give a coherent answer to many a question. Therefore, the author has taken the tourist's route, and by aid of the lamps most recently provided, has tried to show the ancient buildings in this illumination. In describing them with sufficient detail, as she hopes, to make the book useful in each place, she has told the stories of these ruins, endeavoring to put the life into each, and to show the special idea each stands for in the history of Egypt and in the development of the theological thought of the world.

At the same time, though it is not a guide-book, the author trusts this little volume may be found a very thorough guide to Karnak, the centre of Egypt, both in historical and religious importance.

"Before the Temple" is a survey of the religious organization of Egypt, which story suggests the true significance of the Temple; in "The House of Amon" will be found the separate stories of the Empire kings; and in the "Message" from Abydos, Edfu, and Philae,—the sacred places of the Osirian worship,—the inner message of Egypt to the world.

The author's thought is based especially upon the historical facts given to the English-speaking world by the translations and history of Prof. J. H. Breasted, who has worked with the German Egyptologists, and by the explorations and profound researches of Prof. Wm. Flinders Petrie, to both of whom the present writer acknowledges her deep indebtedness:—to Breasted for historical facts and sequences, and to Petrie for the characters and history of the gods. She is also indebted for the story of the finding of the Pharaohs to Canon Rawnsley's account. Others also, among them Budge, Brugsch-Bey and Ebers, have helped to reveal Egypt to her.

In spelling the proper names, Breasted's simple renderings have been generally adhered to. The Egyptians spelled only with consonants, thus allowing some latitude to the imagination of our age in filling in the vowel sounds. Ikhnaton, Khuenaten and Akhetaten are the same; Thutmose, Thothmes, and Tahutimi. Those who have read much of Egypt will find their friends under one set of these forms. The arrangement itself of the Egyptian syllables is not always certain, and some well-known names are recognizable by their terminations as Greek translations, such as Amenophis for the more accruately Egyptian Amenhotep. In this connection it may be interesting to note that a discovery of cuneiform tablets on the site of the capital city of the Hittites, has thrown new light upon this matter of pronunciation, as also do the earlier found Tell-el-Amarna letters which contain the names of Egyptian kings. Among the Hittite tablets is the treaty with Ramese II, of which we have long known the Egyptian copy on the Karnak wall. Its rendering, according to "Egypt and Western Asia in the Light of Recent Researches," comes near to our old pronunciation of Rameses' long name, and seems to indicate that Prof. Maspero's and also the German system of restored pronunciation are neither of them quite right. We shall probably never be absolutely sure. But fortunately, some method of shortening is used by all modern writers, from Greece onward, for the names of these kings; just

INTRODUCTION

as the kings of the present day are called but by one of their many appellations. The full name of the great Rameses as we popularly know him, was User Maat-Ra-setep-en-Ra-Ra-meri-su-meri-Amen, or as others give the first part, Setepnere, Re or Ra signifying the same god.

With earnest appreciation of a meaning in Egypt, the author presents this review of her Nile journey, for which she has chosen from the most important, those things which are typical, or which were necessary to the working out of her thought. When all the details possible have been seen, and when the quiet time comes after, much drops away and is lost in the sweep of the great desert, while from the distance those things of great significance stand out. When we come to think it over, from our individual standpoints, we ask ourselves two questions: What has made the greatest impression? And what did it all mean? For we must all be able to give an answer in order to satisfy ourselves, and to have some expression, some outlet, for the wonder which oppresses our souls. This little volume is the answer one traveller has made to these questions. If it help to grace another's journey, to make Egypt more clear or coherent for another, it will have served its purpose.

M. E. C.

Paris, December, 1913.

CONTENTS

CHAPTER		PAGE
I.	The Desert	19
II.	On the Threshold	24
III.	Egypt, the Dawn	33
IV.	The River	45
V.	From the Love Story of Egypt	64
VI.	Before the Temple	88
VII.	The House of Amon	102
VIII.	The Valley of the Shadow	134
IX.	The City of the King	142
X.	Israel in Egypt	155
XI.	The Evening and the Morning	183
XII.	A Message from the Holy Places	193
XIII.	The Haunt of Horus	204
XIV.	The Gift of Egypt	214
XV.	Light	231

ILLUSTRATIONS

	TO FACE PAGE
A Nubian Vender of Trinkets	Frontispiece
The Day's Last Load	20
The Carriage of the Khedive	26
The Most Important University of Mohammedanism	30
The Modern City	40
The Boats by the Edge of the River	50
A Shadouf	58
The River at Thebes	66
Out of the Past Come Figures	80
The Family in Egypt	96
A Nile Village	120
Our Rowers in the Lock	136
Egyptian Sugar Cane and Humble Egyptian Homes	156
Down by the River	180
Our Villa	200
Water Jars	220

OUT OF EGYPT

OUT OF EGYPT

CHAPTER I

The Desert

IT is the desert—one cannot say the centre of the desert, or its heart, for there seem no boundaries. At first all is without form and void, it is that which lies back of the Beginning. We may speak of the desert expression of Egypt, though the desert has many expressions; for, while sometimes interrupted by the whirlwind, they all seem the expressions of one reverie; which reaches its height at noon when life is fullest and stillest, and we wait breathless for what is to come. Then do we feel how God thought, and the world is.

From this mood we lift up our eyes to the hills which give us one background, and we realize they are not of the shifting sand, but their foundations are sure. They are, in truth, the oldest hills, first to be raised above the waters, and though they are all barren, among them are cool purple shades, "the shadow of a great rock in a thirsty land."

Under the spell it casts upon us, we journey in the desert. Motion incarnate is the camel, stepping so softly that as we ride, it is the earth which seems to reel, yet in the throes of creation. At last before us rise the first and greatest monuments of Man, announcing the beginning of Time where they first marked Space; and deep in a hollow, lifting itself from the drifting sands, we find Form emerging, clothing Majesty—a human head.

Still, after the brief span of human history, it represents the mystery, which we have called by name. For that Time and Space and Form might be, one more thing is essential, the Word—the name of each. Without this word, in the days of dawn men felt that nothing could exist, and further believed that the knowledge of a name gave power over its owner; since the name is the word for the idea of the thing, and thus represents its soul.

But this word is not the Sphinx's secret. We had recognized its name ourselves, ere we learned that the god for whom it stood, is thus addressed in a hymn of the Egyptians:

"O *Form*, one, creator of all things, O one, only, maker of existences."

Uncovered from the sands, as its inscriptions tell us, by an early ruler in obedience to a dream; and gazing into the morning with wide, unseeing eyes through the centuries, what mystery of primitive religion, what revelation of Truth, does the Sphinx embody?

Below its feet, in the shadow of the Pyramids, where the river brings life to the desert, the women of Egypt draw water.

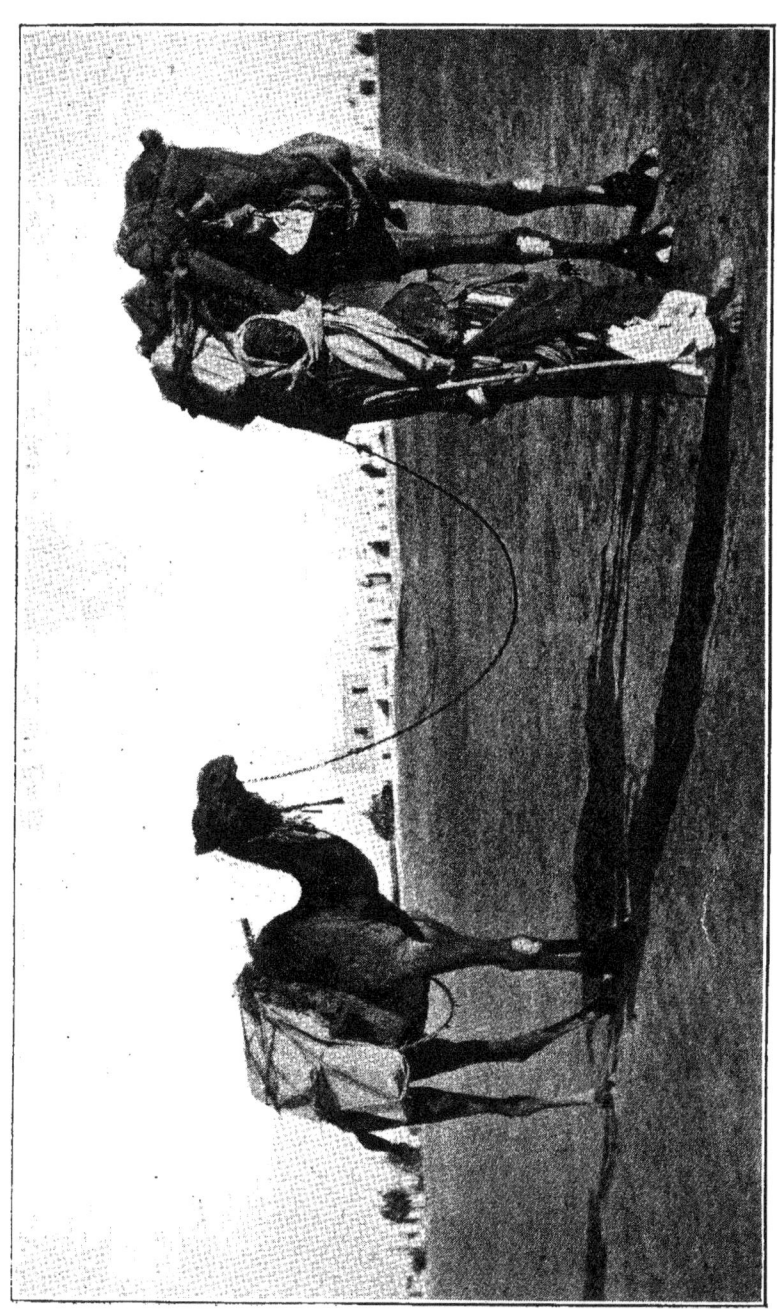

THE DAY'S LAST LOAD

The melancholy note of a large bird calls from the valley; small wagtails flit by us; and a Semitic Bedouin boy in white comes flying from Nowhere on a gaunt camel, waving his arms in sheer exuberance of life. Near us, a company of graceful children, clad each in one loose garment, are busily carrying away the earth to uncover some further marvel of the morning of Time.

We stand beside the Sphinx, with the sun behind us now, and follow its gaze across the tender green of the Nile plain; over the shimmer of the river; over the modern city, to the hills rose-colored in the evening light. Those are the hills from which these first great monuments were wrested—the hills of our first delight. We know that tonight trains of camels are carrying down the day's last load of stone from the edge of the ancient quarries to the boats by the river bank. It is over there, in that continuation of the desert, that One Other and I have taken up our abode, there where the yellow sands sweep round us, and the heavens open above these distant Pyramids for the golden afterglow.

*

Back in our village Helouan, from dawn until "the purple earthshadow climbs the mellow-eastern sky,"* we watch the changes in the Mokattam Hills. After dark itself has fallen, comes a lifting

*R. Talbot Kelly.

of the curtain, and the second glow shines out fine and strange, like the light from a golden lamp; while the rock seems to glow from within. Here, shut from all the world, yet with all space about us, we are daily learning the meanings of what we have seen and heard.

Our villa, the salemlik of an Eastern palace, lies in a garden. The garden is an artificial oasis, but in it the desert blossoms, and nowhere else is the rose so precious. The few houses are the color of the sand, from which they seem hardly separated, reflecting the sunsets in the same way. Some of these buildings are harems, bound round with this monotony of sand. By degrees it is the details which we notice—every rider, every black-robed figure, stands out strongly, till in isolated bits we spell the Present, the ephemeral, eternal life of today, in which we are to have our part. Curious topsy-turvydom, strange anomaly of ancient and modern, East and West. There is much in the situation to amuse us, much which seems irreconcilable.

It is modern life, our Western civilization, which intrudes itself from the hotel to our villa and flutters over the great expanse of desert. "My first horse-back ride was on an elephant," said the very large American woman; "my second, on a camel; my third, on a donkey." For us, the saddles are now often on the donkeys, two little brothers, named Black Diamond and Little Joe respectively.

Little Joe is long and lean, and shows in particular the trait supposed to be most characteristic. His obstinacy will allow no other donkey to get ahead of him. When Black Diamond steps up, Little Joe steps out, and gaining with his long stride, heads my donkey off. Neither persuasion nor force can turn his head. Black Diamond, with good nature, but a like obstinacy, tries again; and so we zigzag fom side to side of the road, a process which rather accelerates our arrival, since we make up by the impetus of the racing impulse, for the extra ground covered.

On the broad desert, however, Black Diamond has a chance. From our saddles the Other and I feel the freedom and charm of the free, golden desert, where even lowly Egyptians walk with the sweep of Victory.

CHAPTER II

On the Threshold

IT was at Cairo, three full moons ago, that we began our journey into the far land of Egypt —Cairo, the new life of Memphis, the city of Saladin's Citadel, and Aladdin's wonderful lamp, the portal to the passage which leads to the Beginning.

Here we were initiated to the spirit of the land, to the poetry and symbolism of the East, by the Mahmal celebration attending the starting of the Mecca caravan. Once every year pilgrims from Cairo, with others gathered from many lands, go on their long journey to bring refreshment from the fountain of the most wide-spread religion in the world, Mohammedanism; and in the open square of the city, where the ceremonies took place, we saw the Orient rise to life as by some magic of the Arabian Nights.

The setting was historic. Before us towered the Citadel of Saladin. Whoever may be the Mohammedans' greatest romantic hero and representative to themselves,—perhaps it is Haroun-ar-Rashid,— Saladin is the most romantic figure and the finest representative of El-Islam to Christendom. For it was Christendom with which, as concentrated in its Crusades, he contended for the little Kingdom of Jerusalem. At that time he proved his knightly qualities by his kindness to his enemy, Richard, the Lionhearted, to whom, as the old story is told, he sent snow from the mountains when Richard lay ill of a fever. The story at least typifies the spirit of the East. Such courtesies, as well as many other things in the Oriental civilization, were then beyond the comprehension of youthful Europe; and the Crusaders took back many ideas more valuable to them than the pathetic little kingdom, surrounded by the desert of an unknown religion, which they abandoned to those sweeping sands hundreds of years ago.

In the story of the Citadel of Cairo is compassed much of the story of Mohammedanism.

The height is now crowned by the Mosque of Mohammed Ali, founder of the reigning dynasty. It was built early in the last century and is copied from the great mosque of Constantinople, the present capital of the Mohammedan world.

At the foot of the Citadel, on the occasion of this Mahmal celebration, was placed the throne of the Khedive. And close beside us stood the sacred camel, waiting to receive the Mahmal, which is the gold-embroidered canopy that symbolizes royalty. How still he stood, the proudest of all camels, never used but for these holy journeys; with what strange silence he received his burden; while a cordon of soldiers closed around him to protect him from too many touches of the thronging crowd of faithful, and thus incidentally, to prevent the faithful from obtaining too many blessings! One old man fought desperately and persistently to reach him. Again and again the soldiers thrust the seeker back, and the master of ceremonies rode up threateningly on his white horse. At last all was ready—battalions of soldiers stood waiting, the attendant camels in gorgeous trappings were mounted, and all were motionless—except that two of the animals turned their heads slowly and observantly, and chewed reminiscently. Even the dervish water and lemonade-carriers and the cake-boys who had moved among the throng, became transfixed with expectancy. Everything awaited the arrival of the Khedive.

Suddenly the band struck up, four white-robed runners dashed into view on the further side of the square, a four-horse carriage drew up before the throne,—and the Khedive had come. The lines of soldiers widened to form an avenue for the camels; and to monotonous, rhythmic, Arab music the procession started, the long rhythmic stride of the Mahmal-bearer scarcely swaying the canopy. Around in a circle some four times they passed, then crossed to the Khedive that he might kiss the rope of the sacred camel, and went out at the farther side.

There followed an imposing review of the Egyptian army, some of whom were to escort the caravan. Then the carriages drove away; and, when the guards were released, the crowd surged over

THE CARRIAGE OF THE KHEDIVE, FOOT OF CITADEL

the square, as a mighty rush of water when a dam is broken. Not a foot of ground in that great open space, so ample for the review, was now visible. It was the annual religious flood-tide in the people's lives.

This is Egypt, this is Mohammedanism.

Strains and fragments of its poetry recur through the modern life of Cairo. The beautiful white-robed runners, the short-lived Sais, precede the carriages; veiled and black-robed women move about, carrying their naked babies astride their shoulders, as did Egyptian women of old. And water-carriers are everywhere:—some with the skins of unfiltered Nile water; others with jars of filtered water on their backs, from which by bending, they may pour the liquid over their shoulders into little cups; and still others with large glass bottles slung before them containing lemonade.

These water-carriers are all dervishes, but we see nothing here or in their ceremonies of this religious aspect of their lives. The ceremonies of the howling and dancing dervishes to which foreigners are admitted are but a travesty upon their genuine religion.

As we followed the crowd back into the town, we realized how two architectural beauties mark the background of this Eastern life—everywhere the lacy, heaven-aspiring minarets and the fast vanishing "mashrabiyeh" windows. The name given to these beaded woodwork windows signifies "place of water" and was originally applied only

to that projecting portion where the water was set to keep cool. They have their romance too, these windows, since they form the screened balconies through which the women peer down upon the world. Unfortunately, much of the woodwork has now been stripped from the houses and carried away bodily to make screens in Western homes.*
This denudes Cairo of one of its chief graces—and under the present law the balconies may not be replaced for fear of fire.

One still sees in the bazaars the fascinating equipment of Eastern life; alluring because that life is so hidden from us, and the possession of its externals seems to give an entrance to it, at least, suggests its mysteries. But it is to be regretted that most of the contact of Europeans with natives is through bargaining—a most superficial contact and often entirely without understanding on the part of the Westerners, who condemn what they consider Oriental dishonesty. Yet they themselves do not seriously object to getting a bargain; why should they be disturbed at the Oriental attempt to make one? To the credit of the native be it said that it is a game which he enjoys most when his adversary comprehends it. Europeans and Americans are prone to treat other peoples with a superior contempt which does not facilitate understanding. The Oriental has a different standard of right and wrong, but he has his own

---

*The hotels in Egypt possess beautiful examples. Mena House has the finest collection.

ON THE THRESHOLD 29

deep sense of honor. His simple and childlike intensity of feeling is accompanied and safe-guarded by a profound reserve. It often leads him to display the opposite of his true self,—as Lane makes clear,—and few indeed, among the students of the Orient, has he trusted sufficiently to admit them to the secrets of his inner life.

The bazaars of Cairo do not compare with those of Tunis, which is a far more Oriental city. Yet they suggest the Arabian Nights; and the building in which we found the chief of them, charmed us with a spell far different and deeper. For the narrow street runs through the Khan-el-Khalil, a house of the same idea as the khan or inn at Bethlehem—the first kind of hotel, a building into which the caravans of olden time came and were unloaded. The goods were placed on the ground floor and sold there, while the merchants lodged above them. In Mediæval days commerce meant travel and adventure. Venice, the gateway from the East to the West, possesses such a building erected for the merchants, with sculptured camels to indicate its use. Cairo was once full of khans.

It was the Mohammedan Arabs of the Middle Ages who, as a Semitic people, living an Old Testament life, cast upon Egypt and the Egyptians the glamour of the East, and became to Christian Europe which strove with them, a living illustration of the West-adopted Bible story.

In Cairo one finds today the most important university of Mohammedanism in the Mosque of

El-Azhar, with its seven thousand scholars from different parts of the Mohammedan world "all seated on the ground." The students from each country have a room to themselves.

Geography has been introduced into the curriculum only within the last few years. Wonderful is the delight of the teachers in their new appliances; but we were told that students, beholding Cairo as a pin-head on the map of Africa, refuse to believe. Is not Cairo the great centre of the world?—the rest but a small fringe or margin?

It is the study of Koran Arabic and the memorizing of that holy book by writing it, which occupy most of the school life of these youths. The classes, if such they can be called, are innumerable little groups, each about a teacher, the members of each being near of an age. Many a little circle we find of Kindergarten years. Quiet, industrious and subdued under the stern watchfulness of their teachers, the gleam of their eyes reveals their native merriment and life. Is it this quality that keeps them cheery under conditions which our spoiled babies could not survive? They are writing with clumsy little fingers passages of the Koran, or perhaps the ninety-and-nine beautiful names of God, which are for them the beginning of knowledge. This method reminds us of the scholastic period of education in Europe—with this difference, that the motive beneath and through the Mohammedan learning is faith.

It is within the mosques that we see Mohammedanism in its most ideal and poetic aspect.

THE MOST IMPORTANT UNIVERSITY OF MOHAMMEDANISM

ON THE THRESHOLD

Five times a day at hours prescribed and in the eight positions of prayer must the devout Mohammedan praise God. If he is in his little shop in the bazaars and cannot get away to the mosque, he must, at the nearest possible moment to that which is ordained, drop down upon his prayer-rug facing Mecca, and withdrawing his eyes from the world about him, repeat those worshipful expressions which constitute his contemplation of the Universal. It is a curious and suggestive picture. The small open shop is raised somewhat above the ground, so that we commonly sit on the edge of the floor as on a bench, to bargain. At prayer time, the walls form a frame, enclosing the rich background of rugs and Eastern ornaments, and the one white figure, with its look of inner absorption.

But somehow this picture reminds us of that Eastern praying on street corners, once so simply and so strongly condemned.

In the mosque, it is different, when the worshippers, having bathed hands and feet like the Hebrew priests of old, at the holy fountain of ablutions in the court, walk barefoot on to the holy ground and seem to enter into the silence.

The Mosque of Sultan Hassan, in the shadow of the Citadel, is the finest in Cairo. Its magnificent door is perhaps the most exquisite example of Arabic stalactite work in Egypt. But it is the cracked old walls which have for us a peculiar fascination, for this mosque was built from the

Great Pyramid. We know that those old stones were quarried thousands of years ago, near our present abiding-place; were taken across to the western side of the river, and over the hard road of the pyramid builder to be an inner coating of the mighty tomb of Cheops. Memphis faded when the glory of Alexandria arose; and later, the ancient city was destroyed that the stones of Memphis might become Cairo on the eastern river-bank. Then these blocks were retransported to receive new life—I had almost said, to enclose the latest chapter in the story of the ancient building; but the mosque is already tottering, and the Pyramid will continue to be when the beautiful Mohammedan temple has perished.

In our imagination the crumbling walls already fall apart and we pass through the portal of the East, back toward the Beginning of the West.

CHAPTER III

Egypt, the Dawn.

AS in the sunset skies and the desert sands the color of barren Egypt is marvellous, so is it with the life of the people. The color is the revelation of Egypt: yellow houses, whose chief beauty is their woodwork; mixed costumes of all colors; dark faces. It is true that the white Semitic Orient of other countries seems to mean a finer development, while it yet speaks of that early stage which possesses spiritual revelation and which belongs to the East. But the color of Egypt is the color of dawn, present now in the sunset,—yea, it is the color out of which the white light of eternal day is made.

It was the Past which drew us in the stones of Cairo, yet the way back seemed long at first. We felt that we possessed a clue for ourselves when we could decipher a few hieroglyphic signs. So each individual may have the feeling of a discoverer. Gradually the Past absorbed us, until Egypt belonged to the ancient Egyptians—all that has happened since seemed accident and impertinence. The magnitude of the Past overcame us, and a magic drew us into the spirit of those far-off times.

Egypt, from Cairo to Philae, the Gem of the Nile,—Egypt is the museum of the world, with a poetry of symbolism in a romance of stories which clings to it all. Those stories form part of the foundation of our own. The museum in Cairo is Egypt's heart, where are now gathered together and protected the mystic treasures which are found: jewelry of queens and princesses; scarabs with the names of kings; papyri; gods and goddesses; and the ushabtis, "little answerers," figures of servants buried with the dead, so that when the spirit is called to work in the Afterworld, they may answer for him, "Here am I!"

What poetry we find in the Egyptian titles: "The Book of Portals" and the "Book of that which is in the Underworld!" The Egyptian idea of the Ka or double, with its sign of the uplifted arms was as the Hindoos' "Astral body;" and their thought of the after-life, like that of the Mohammedans today, was the thought of a long journey.

Wonderful old Egyptians, who divided Time into our calendar, long before history began; who measured the hours of the day and night and saw a symbol for each; who first wrote of the seven ages of Man! Back through Rome and Greece, without a break, we can trace in Egypt the beginnings of our science, of our material civilization. And beyond all this there is something, formal still, but more profound than all.

There came a moment when, in the royal room

EGYPT THE DAWN

of the museum we gazed face to face upon the Pharaohs. That is where the spell was laid upon our own lives, through our deepest feeling. Here, with his strong, still, old face uncovered, is the second Rameses, Rameses, the Great, father of Pharaoh's daughter. Merneptah, his son, the Pharaoh of the Exodus, is also here, but his body has never been unwrapped. Because of the Hebrew story, there are those who refuse to believe that it is he, and we know that his own tomb appears as if unused. But the Israelites made their record after looking from the other side of the waters in a moment of intense excitement and relief. There is every reason to suppose that Egyptian troops may have been overwhelmed in the sand at the head of the Red Sea, but Merneptah was not with them and escaped.

These, then, are the Pharaohs, whose story was told us when, in our own form of religion, inculcated in childhood, we were taught reverence. And the deeper we advance into this mysterious land, the more in its broadest sense do we realize that religion is the secret of Egypt, the secret of the Beginning.

Under the spell which conquered the interest of the Present, we visited again and yet again the Pyramids.

Bronze lions guard the entrance to the bridge, over which, while it was closed against the river traffic, we passed in the midst of carriages, laden camels, wide-panniered, jostling donkeys, and pedestrians. From a garden at the other end, a tram carried us along the beautiful road. This road was constructed for the pilgrimage of the Empress Eugénie to these wonders of ancient Egypt at the time when the Khedive Ismail built Ghezireh Palace for her reception, and when he entertained her with such splendid fêtes as the world has scarcely seen and only an Oriental imagination could conceive. But a Western world was obliged to take charge of the financial side of Ismail's affairs, and Ismail died, broken-hearted, in exile in Constantinople. The Empress Eugénie, bereaved in a different way of her empire,—of her husband and her son, wanders sometimes in her dahabieh up the Nile and through the land of Egypt. Ghezireh Palace is an hotel, and this road of proud remembrance is the highway of the camel of the Bedouin and the carriage of the European. Occasionally a horse appears in gorgeous Oriental trappings. The tramway runs along one side of the way under a row of magnificent trees; and thus we approached the first to be built and the last to survive of the Seven Wonders of the World. We dropped the Present when we stood beneath it—the Great Pyramid—overwhelmed by its size and the fineness of its masonry.

Such piles of stone, royal Mountains of Man, rise, breaking the desert for twenty miles on the western side of the river, but this Ghizeh group alone are "The Pyramids" to us all. They are an ennead standing for a dynasty, though only the three largest are generally known.

EGYPT THE DAWN

The position, the proportions, and the relations to one another of these three pyramids, reveal remarkable knowledge of direction, geometry, and principles of construction; they fill us now with amazement at the methods by which in that non-mechanical age, such prodigious weights were handled. As the outcome of their revelations, the Pyramids have furnished material for whole chapters, and even volumes, upon their secret significance. With what amount of conscious knowledge of occult meanings, these buildings were constructed, we can hardly know, but that which is true must prove mathematically true in all the larger knowledge of relations by which it may be tested. Therefore the Great Pyramid is considered by some a key to the whole philosophy of sacred numeration.

We stand where centuries of golden sand have beat about its base, slowly or swiftly have drifted or swept on it, and after all surged softly past. And it rests firm, a universal symbol, for us to read and comprehend at last.

The Egyptians, the first historic nation, and the first nation of the West, with whom lay our earliest beginnings of objective knowledge, here expressed their own strong sense of the material realm, the world of *Form*. Here they raised at the Beginning, "the most stupendous mass of masonry ever put together by human hands;" for it must cast the longest shadow over Time. It marks for us our entrance to the Past.

However, the Pyramid not only expresses this particular idea, but the Old Kingdom itself at its height. As Breasted suggests, it is the early state, here wrought into a tomb, beneath the apex of a single block. For the nation belonged to the king, whose control was absolute, with his sons and the members of his family next beneath him, their lives all given to making a material "eternal house" for the body of the great king who was to them a god. Thus the Old Kingdom has perpetuated itself.

Through all the changing hours of the long day the Pyramids stand the same, yet different. We loved them best in the evening light, when, free from the distractions of donkeys and guides, we slipped around the corner of the greatest, and went south, along the path between it and its family of three. Beyond these, looking along the valley and the desert plateau, we saw, as it were, a vast amphitheatre of sand, smooth as a circular sweep of snowdrift. In a hollow below us, perpetually arising through the earth was that majestic human head. We went down before the Sphinx, seeking its mystery which is never fully revealed.

Strange stories cluster round this head. It is not the Woman of the Greeks, but once represented a finite human king and then a god. Its inscriptions tell how Thutmose IV of the eighteenth dynasty dreamed of, discovered, and uncovered it from the sands. And it is still surreptitiously appealed to.

Just beyond it is a temple, sometime known as the Temple of the Sphinx, but now discovered to be only the giant gateway to the Second Pyramid. We look down into it, as it lies excavated, and realize what a Past is buried here. This gate was on the edge of the desert plateau, so that in floodtime boats came to its steps. From it, as from the others, belonging to the other Pyramids, the white-robed priests entered an inclined and covered causeway, leading up to the Pyramid enclosure. And all was white—gate and causeway and royal tomb,—save when lighted golden by the Sun. The king, whom the people wrought for, but rarely caught a glimpse of, was to them a god. Authority was from the first supposed to be divine.

The people dwelt in Memphis, the "White Wall," below. Upon a day we visited its site. That capital of the Ancient Empire and largest city of the New—Memphis of five thousand years and millions of inhabitants—is gone like the grass of the field—gone, to be endowed with new life in the city across the river.

In a lonely palm grove, where once stood the magnificent temple of Ptah, is the only representative of Memphis in her living glory—Rameses II, in two great prostrate statues. They unlock for us the story of Egypt; their loneliness is full of significance. It is Rameses, who, more than any other, represents the whole of Egypt, not only in the greatness of his reign and achievements, but in his connection with the Hebrews. He stands for one stage in the development of Man, Moses stands for the next.

Perhaps in no country of the world is history so personal, so completely included in the lives of the rulers. We are personally interested because much that belongs to our own lives had its source in Egypt; and the stories of the kings are spread out before us as an open book along the Nile,—in statues, in inscriptions, in paintings, in the very bodies themselves. The life of Rameses, the Rameses of Hebrew story, is revealed to us in detail almost from the day of his birth.

Time in Egypt is reckoned by the lives of kings; and in those early ages the mass of the people, being practically slaves, did only the will of the ruler and were truly included in his life. In Rameses, more than any other, is summed up the whole genius of Egypt at its height. He stands for his country, not only in his own period, but through all periods after, and for all time. It is the "Land of Rameses."

Memphis is gone, save for the great king, who, prostrate, merely rests, serene and unconquerable in his green grove, bearing the image of his favorite daughter, Bent-Anat, on his side. Time enough has passed for everything to drop away from him here, yet he remains alone, and all the greater for that loneliness.

Ptah, the pylons of whose huge temple, behind the figures Petrie unearthed in 1909-1910, was Rameses' favorite deity and was one of the oldest

THE MODERN CITY

and most venerated of the Egyptian gods. It was "he who not only made the germ of life, but its conditions and laws, he who was beginner and beginning." In him they saw the father of men and of their gods. His high-priesthood was a high honor in Egypt, often held by the kings' sons. One of Rameses' own older sons bore it; and a younger one, Merneptah, who reigned after him, was named for Ptah.

Though the Egyptian priests became initiated to some conception of a universal god, they taught the people to see his attributes under various tangible forms, and each priesthood claimed supremacy for the particular form it served. To the Egyptian people the idea of divinity personified by Ptah, dwelt in the Sacred Bull, which bore certain curious and definite markings. When one of these bulls died, his successor, to be recognized by the markings, was searched for and was sure to be found.

Ptah was always represented by the figure of the bull. No wonder the Israelites, living as they had in the Delta country to which Memphis was the key, could not feel at home when they went out into the wilderness without a golden calf!

Rameses himself had been in the north as a youth. When he was a king, and his campaigns called him into the northeast, he lived almost entirely in the Delta country, to be nearer the field of action. This explains the story of the finding of Moses by Rameses' young daughter near the university city of On or Heliopolis, which Rameses sometimes used as a residence instead of Memphis. Finally, he placed his capital at Tanis, near the north-eastern border, that he might in person guard the gate to his dominion. Of the two recently discovered treasure cities* in the Delta, built of bricks of Nile mud, and believed, according to the Hebrew traditions, to have been constructed by them for Rameses, one city bears his name; and a brick, now in the Berlin Museum, is inscribed with the same cartouche, "User-Maat-Ra-setep-en-Ra," the prenomen which we learn to know so well. The making of bricks was the Israelites' task, and the order to "make bricks without straw," or, more accurately, to find the straw which was no longer provided and still to produce the same number of bricks, was the oppression which caused the Hebrews finally to rise and move out. Thus they became a nation. Is not that brick as the cornerstone of a new order?

To the south of the Temple of Ptah, Petrie excavated in 1909-1910, the huge palace of Apries, the Pharaoh Hophra of the Bible, one of the latest kings of Egypt. But the palace was built upon others, a veritable store-house, going down to the earliest times.

Beyond Memphis is the village of Sakkara, near which is the re-opened tomb of the Sacred Bulls of Ptah, where the footprints of workmen who closed a vault thousands of years ago were found

*Raameses and Pithom. Exodus I:2.

EGYPT THE DAWN 43

in the sand inside—a thing so intimate, so fleeting as to be almost spiritual, preserved through centuries, to vanish, liberated, at a breath. One of the names of Ptah, was Ptah Sakkar-Osiris, the God of the Dead, literally the Opener; "who bestows on the departed sun its power of rising again, and on departed souls a resurrection to eternal life on the other side of the grave."* Today the little Arab village of Sakkara existing on a part of the ancient cemetery, unwittingly bears his name; and many tombs have been opened near by. Back of the Empire, back of the Middle Kingdom, it was the Ancient Kingdom which was buried here many centuries before Rameses, and was treasured up for us in this great Necropolis, which includes the Pyramids and extends for twenty miles on the western edge of the desert. Here is the first great effort in stone, the Step-Pyramid, a lasting memorial to that early architect who built it for King Zoser, "the great wise man Imhotep," who could interpret the king's dream in reference to a seven years' famine and who was remembered as a god twenty-five hundred years afterward; here, too, is the tomb of Ptahhotep, the man who wrote the oldest known book, a book of precepts; here, the "eternal house" of Ti, the first record of a self-made man. Ti rose from the ranks and attained to the hand of a princess, and his children bore the rank of princes. His statue is in the museum of Cairo.

The sands have drifted over these tombs of the
*Ebers

Ancient Kingdom, whose guest chambers were originally small houses built above the ground. The mummy-chambers underneath were bare, as were the shafts which led to them, and the latter were filled with rock to insure the safety of the body. We went down into the guest-chambers, whose walls are decorated with fine reliefs. It is the earth-life that is imaged here, the whole life of the period: hunting, ship-building, agriculture, the bringing of the produce of his fields to the master of the house. We find that then, as now, girls carried the burdens on their heads.

One may linger long in this life of the Ancient Kingdom, to which one finds entrance only through a tomb.

CHAPTER IV

The River

STILL under the power of the Past we returned to Cairo, and set sail up the river which leads into the Realm of the Ages, the way that kings and princesses once went. On that night of our departure the modern city, with its palaces and palms, slipped from our sight. And then at last Egypt was another dream fulfilled—at sunset, when dreams come true. We have seen how this river, the life of Egypt, is the color of the heaven from which it comes; while the barren, yellow cliffs that edge the desert on both sides of the valley take on soft shades of rose and are reflected in the water; and the ravines are shadows of purple and blue which give depth and expression to the constant face of Nature.

It is the setting we think we should imagine if we did not know of it, for that brilliant civilization, crude in some respects but full of color, which developed here.

On the second day we came to Beni-Hassan. Donkeys carried us through palm groves and green fields and along the line where the Nile soil meets the sand. At the foot of steep cliffs we dismounted to climb, far up and back, to the shelf where the precious dead had been laid away more than four thousand years ago; laid away with the greatest care at the bottom of pits sunk fifty feet deep which were closed and filled with stones. We understand what the Hebrews meant when they talked of "going down into the pit!" The rock chambers above, which we entered, were the places where friends would meet to keep the memories.

Before one of these tombs, that of Khnumhotep, are two pre-Doric columns, interesting architectural milestones of human progress. As the tombs admitted us to the Old Kingdom at Memphis, so here we gain entrance between these pillars to the Middle Kingdom. The strange frescoes on the walls of the guest chambers are a priceless record, opened to be read and learned, and now fading fast away. Each tomb is a book containing a life or the story of a campaign—one chapter in the history of Egypt. The scenes from the life of the deceased,—generally a prince or governor—and the inscriptions, supply many facts and details of existence and of historical events in Egypt, in the days of those kings under whom these princes ruled. Among the records are contracts for the keeping up of the tombs and the bringing of flowers on certain days. The most sacred place, the niche walled up at the end of the guest chamber, contained that which was cherished most, next to the body of the beloved one—his portrait statue. Might not his very spirit, as they believed, take possession of it? What can we, in these days of psychical research, deny? We feel a sacrilege in looking on those mutilated statues, whose proteeting wall is broken down, only less than one must feel in looking upon the actual Pharaohs.

These tombs have also their connected family story. Khnumhotep was a partisan of Amenemhet I, the general who gained possession of the throne, and ushered in the Twelfth Dynasty, the classic dynasty of the Middle Kingdom. Khnumhotep was count of the city of Menet-Khufu, from whence had come Pharaoh Khufu, dynasties before. This count succeeded also to the Oryx-nome,—a nome being one of the principal divisions of Egypt, and he, its ruler, a nomarch. He was the father of Ameni and of Nakht, who were by special favor of the son of Amenemhet, Sesostris I, appointed to inherit their father's "fiefs," Ameni as governor of the Oryx-nome, Nakht as count of Menet-Khufu. Beket, the sister of these two, married the vizier, who was also governor of the residence city. The son of Beket and the vizier, later Khnumhotep II, was appointed by the king to succeed his uncle Nakht as count of Menet-Khufu. He, realizing that his succession came through his mother, whose position as the daughter of a nomarch was regarded as of much importance by the Pharaoh, himself sought in marriage the heiress of the Jackal-nome.

As we go down through the history of Egypt we shall find the importance of the mother and the daughter in the Pharaonic succession itself and even in the temple orders.

One picture in the tomb of Khnumhotep lingers in our memories. It is a group of foreigners, evidently a Semitic people, bringing gifts,—and was at first popularly supposed to represent the entry of Joseph's brethren into Egypt. But it is now known to belong to a time before Abraham was. Nevertheless it signifies for us the entrance of that Semitic element which so strongly influenced the development of Egypt. This race was in power during the Hyksos period, when Israel's children are supposed to have come in. That would account for their welcome. In a deeper sense than appears on the surface, a later dynasty "knew not Joseph."

We were yet more impressed by an inscription within another tomb. Wonderful it was in Cairo to gaze upon the face of Pharaoh Rameses, asleep more than three thousand years. But more wonderful to hear the voice which speaks to us from the walls of Ameni's tomb, a voice silent more than four thousand years, but telling us now of a standard, not merely of right, but of goodness, in that far off time, which we today feel more important to know than anything in that early civilization.

"I have never made the daughter of a poor man to grieve; I have never defrauded the widow;" Ameni, the governor tells us, "I have never oppressed the laborer, . . . there was never a

THE RIVER

person in want in my time, and no one went hungry during my rule, for if years of leanness came, I made them to plough up all the arable land in the nome—up to its very frontiers on the north and south. Thus I kept its people alive and obtained for them provisions. To the widow I gave the same amount as I gave to her who had a husband, and I made no distinction between the great and the little in all that I gave. And afterwards, when the Nile floods were high, and wheat and barley and all things were abundant, I made no addition to the amounts due from them."*

Because of this inscription, the dark portal of that dim tomb chamber on the desert cliff is the doorway for us to a knowledge of the spirit of Ameni's time.

A straight, steep path from the terrace dropped us again to the plain and the present day. We rode back in the sunshine, trailing clouds of golden dust, until we reached the grateful cool of the palm grove, and the little white steamer awaiting us.

Further up the Nile, our going through the lock of the great dam at Assiut, proved an interesting procedure. Thousands of years ago, the Egyptians regulated the flow of the river. That regulation was lost, and it is only recently, after many ages, that such a work has been accomplished again. The lock is at the side of the great barrage which helps to control the water. Our steamer

*Budge

slid over close to the bank where lay a line of sailboats, filled with human freight. So near we came it seemed as if our projecting paddle-wheels must knock these people off. They got up good-naturedly and shoved; and if our boat had moved off far, a dozen of them would have dropped in the Nile. Presently the water gates before us opened, and out poured a flood of boats, one grain-craft with its idle oar completely covered with birds. Then we moved, with many stops and much shouting from our native pilots—for the lock was barely wide enough to admit our paddle wheels, and the current against us was strong. No sooner were we at rest in the box than in followed the line of boats which had been waiting along the shore for an opening of the gates. Two little fishing-boats somehow slipped under our side, and lay close beneath our bow. Madly our pilot shouted, "Imshi!" ("Go away!") to those behind, unmindful of the push they had given him. They too, unmindful, crowded in, but the foremost moored to rings so far back in the lock, that the last boat, which was towed, could not be drawn inside the limit. The big spar tangled with another, the lower end was thrust over our lower deck, the smaller spar behind caught in the closing gates, Then there was excitement, for these people are like children. At last, by much moving through them all, the little spar was brought in, and the gates closed. The drawbridge swung over above them, and a crowd passed over it. Slowly the

THE BOATS BY THE EDGE OF THE RIVER

THE RIVER

lock filled from beneath, the gates before us began to unclose, and the two little fishing-boats scudded out of danger, while we came lumbering after.

It was such incidents as these which enlivened our trip; for a Nile journey is not only very beautiful—a poetic reverie full of the Past,—it is also very picturesque and full of humor in the Present; and these apparently conflicting elements cause a constant confusion in the mind. Our navigators were natives and clever ones, though we frequently ran aground. But what of that!—it was the will of Allah—and as we did not run at night, there was no danger. As for the captain or manager, he was a dapper little European, who used perfumery, and had nothing to do with the running of the ship. He was there to control the natives and to look after the passengers; and right well he did it, as our excursions have proved. He always rode out to meet us and counted us like sheep, that not one might be missing when the ship sailed.

The second stop in our journey was at Assiut on the western bank. The coming of our boat to these towns and villages seemed to cause as much excitement as must the passing of the boats of former governors or princesses. The people rushed along the bank to be at the landing-stage—swarms of black cloaks against the dusty brown of hill and houses. We were as interested as they, while we watched from our upper deck the loading and unloading going on below, and the transactions between native vendors of bread and fruit and our native passengers.

It is here at Assiut, among the rock-tombs similar to those of Beni-Hassan, that records have been sought of the Ninth and Tenth Dynasties. These rulers followed the Two Lost Dynasties, of which we have no records, since they began in an Age of Terror, that broke up the Old Kingdom. The feudal nobles of this place were prominent adherents of the Ninth and Tenth Pharaonic Houses. Here too, is a family story: the daughter of the nomarch widowed, her little son educated at the Pharaoh's court while she, succeeding her father, ruled for the boy till he came of age.

The old Assiut is now the capital and largest town of Upper Egypt, and was for long the end of an important caravan route. We took a carriage instead of donkeys for the long drive to the town and through the bazaars. Part of the place is like any Southern city, with a long avenue of lebbek trees; part is built, like all the native villages, of bricks of Nile mud. Before the door of one of the huts sat a woman churning something in a skin, her naked brown baby beside her. Some of these dark children are quite beautiful, and full of mischief. They did not trouble us if treated kindly— a smile was worth as much as bakshish. Little girls ran after us, crying a peculiar call, a number of syllables in quick succession. Some of the children carried kids to show us, the youngest gleefully turning the animals' heads, which all

THE RIVER 53

baaed as they came around to position, exactly like the toys in our shops at home.

Of course the people are dirty and their clothes are dirty—all of a piece. But somehow one does not mind—at a distance. They seem like well-worn dolls, whose clothes are not meant to come off. It was explained to us how the women skillfully change their dresses over their heads while bathing in the river. The very religion of the Egyptians necessitates much washing of hands and feet, while the earth dirt is kind and itself disinfects. They are lightly clothed and live in the pure open air. The question of the flies and the babies' eyes is the most serious one.

This condition is being slowly met by the medical mission work. There is a large American mission school and hospital at Assiut. The American and English mission work seems admirably organized in Egypt, with the intention not to interfere, but to educate and heal, to train for cleanliness and morality. No vain attempt is made to disaffect the women in their inferior position; but, among the higher class of men, English university graduates strive to create the desire for a better position for the native women. These college men prepare the way for the women missionaries' work

Our ride through the bazaars was chiefly occupied in bargaining for an Assiut scarf. These charming shimmering pieces, known all over the West as Egyptian scarves, are made by the women here—supposedly for bridals,—and, with the red pottery, are the specialties of the town. Our carriage, accompanied by a smiling native policeman, was surrounded by merchants, and the bargaining began as we entered the narrow streets and ended with the flinging of the graceful thing into our laps, as we drove out. When we arrived at the side of the steamer, we found brisk bargaining going on there also, prices sinking rapidly as the moment of departure drew near; and purchases were made as long as money and goods could be thrown across the widening strip of water between the Egyptians and their amused and eager customers. In fact, the eagerness of the latter to get a bargain quite equalled that of the sellers themselves. Turkish customers, negotiating with natives, assume an air of supreme indifference.

As we advanced up the river our first temple took us again into the Past. It was the Temple of Dendera. We had read how the building was begun some hundreds of years before the Roman days in Egypt, was finished about the time of Cleopatra, and used through the Roman period; how it and its accompanying outside chapels had become, during the centuries since, gradually buried, until it was merely a hill upon the top of which modern Egyptians had built their houses; and how the authorities in charge of antiquities have cleared away the modern incumbents, and have dug out the temple, casting up the sand in a circle around it, a little distance from its walls and quite as high.

Through fields of Egyptian clover we rode to the spot on donkeys, which strung themselves along the path, as if going to some old festival.

Before us in the desert, beyond the living green plains, appeared a huge, uneven mound of earth. As we approached, it opened; and like something taking shape out of chaos, there rose in the centre, with the earth still clinging to its sides, the perfect temple—a building of wonderfully beautiful proportions, its sculptures seeming not broken, but scarcely finished yet. That was the impression—we had come to witness a resurrection!

Down into the solemn hall we passed, among the giant Hathor pillars, which marked this temple as belonging to a goddess, the personification of Nature; on into the dark ante-chambers and the corridors, marvelling at the massiveness of the building, marvelling equally how every inch of its many walls, inside and out, is covered with reliefs —among them the famous Cleopatra; on into the little court and temple in the side, where from the ceiling, the sun shining upon Hathor's head symbolizes the blessing of the temple; and into the holy of holies in the heart of the great building:— feeling more and more deeply the majesty and mystery of the Egyptian priesthood, and the subtlety of the Romans who could recognize the attributes of their own gods under Egyptian names. Into the secrets of the priests we entered, passing down to their subterranean treasure chamber in the thickness of the wall. It still contains the treasure of the temple, reliefs of finest workmanship. We found this place as difficult of access as it well could be. At the back of the farthest chamber of the temple a flight of stairs leads down to a wall in which, some distance above the level of the lowest step is an opening like an oven door. On the other side is a landing, from which, lighted by the candles of the guide, we made our way down more stairs at right angles to the first, leading to a long, narrow, airless passage. It is a passage full of wonders, which flashed upon us and receded into darkness. Every hair of the sculptured heads, every feather of the birds, is perfect. But a sudden alarm seized us. A stout helmeted African-Englishman of our ship's company, had attempted to come down, and though divested of the helmet, which he had left in the charge of some young Turks, he stuck fast in the oven door. Still he would not miss the treasure and somehow dragged himself through, finally liberating us, whom he had penned below.

We were glad to come up after that and to seek the light of day, so we went to the roof, a roof of temples and terraces, upon which, before the resurrection, had stood the Egyptian village. From its highest level we looked over the Nile valley and saw at our feet the small but exquisite birth chapel just emerging from the ground. We descended by the long East stair, dark almost all its length; yet as we held our candles to the wall, we could see that there was with us a great proces-

THE RIVER

sion; and beautiful were the forms and exquisitely moulded the faces of those silent companions. It was the procession for Dendera's festival—the festival of the New Year—which perpetually through all the ages, passes up the East stair and down the West. In modern buildings one may sometimes feel a presence, where one may not see. In these cold halls, one sees.

We passed out of the gate of Dendera and rode away; and we looked back, trying to see it all again—only to find that the temple had vanished, apparently had returned into the earth. But we hold it in our minds, the perfect model, by which to understand and re-construct all the temples of that old religion.

On we passed up the flowing river, so changing yet constant, so full of reflections—the same Nile which was the life of the ancient Egyptians. How beautiful it is, how mysterious! As we gazed upon its surface there was explained to us anew one of Egypt's secrets:—How the Egyptians, unable to look upon the sun, which symbolized God for them under the name of Amon-Re, beheld him in his reflection in the water with his light spread into wings. Is not this the meaning of that Winged Sun found above the first portal to all Egyptian temples? Were they not the Wings of the Morning?

Over the river, across the reflection of this Winged Sun of all time, float the cross-winged sail-boats of today. On shore, are friendly groups of lebbek trees, and every here and there a terraced cut in the bank where groups of men raise the water in buckets from one level to the next. As we proceed further south, this Shadouf, as it is called, is replaced by the Sakieh, or wheel. A wall of masonry closes the cut beneath the trees. The string of buckets depends from the wheel, and a patient ox is turning it, a cluster of villagers is always about it.

The melancholy creak of the wheel sounds far, till it is thin and musical as an Aeolian harp. It is said that once a wheel was so perfectly put together that it could not creak; but the owner was wroth with the maker and declared that the Sakieh was not perfect for him, since he could not tell whether the boy who kept the ox going was asleep or not.

All this reveals the cause of Egypt's prosperity. The watering of the land is at the root of all her present agriculture, all her ancient civilization, and must still be laboriously done, in spite of canals and dams.

From Cairo to Assouan we could see the modern life of the modern Egyptians forever drawn to the river like its own upper tributaries and carried on its bosom. The stream, cutting through and opening up the land, today causes green fields and forms a highroad for the natives; and at the same time a way for us to see and understand it all. Modern practical industries have been guided and stimulated by the English. Sometimes the real

A SHADOUF

and active life of the Present threatens the destruction of the ideal in the Past, as this ideal exists today in the form of monumental temples; threatens perhaps also the romantic ideal of Egypt in our own minds. It is true that in this Eastern-appearing country was the beginning of our Western civilization; yet it is somehow startling to us now to find the end with the beginning, and to see Occidental industry and bustle in this Orient-colored land.

Truly, Man has travelled far in Egypt.

However, this modern life of Egypt, which itself contains opposite elements, and also conflicts with the old, still receives a double beauty from the Orient and the Past. Near Helouan, we saw how stone is cut beside the mouths of the ancient quarries; and how it is carried on camels to boats beside the Nile. On our journey our studies were occasionally punctuated by the smoke-stacks of a sugar factory, which we took at first for an obelisk. Perhaps the reality jarred upon our sensibilities. Yet the sugar-cane is still carried under picturesque Egyptian sails, and thatches humble Egyptian homes. Egyptian cotton, also, has not only all the superior fineness of a product of the East, but is still associated with the romance of the camel and the caravan.

The products of purely native industries like pottery-making, especially the Egyptian water-jars for Egyptian use—these float down the current and pass us.

The river bears a living Present through the whole of history. The history is evident in the varied human types which throng about us at different stages of our journey. At Cairo there were numerous Turks, a few of whom may be found in official capacities up the Nile. There are not many Arabs. Some we saw as merchants in Cairo, others live their Bedouin life in the desert. Their name is erroneously and popularly applied to the true Egyptians by tourists, perhaps because of the Arabic language and the religion last imposed upon these natives by their erstwhile conquerors, perhaps also because the name seems to cast over them the fascination which the East has always had for the West. After all, religion is before race. But the mass of the inhabitants of Egypt are Egyptians, descendants of that most ancient people. One may often see, in guide or rower, a startling resemblance to the bronze features of Seti I in the museum. While the Arabs always retain their graceful native costume, the better class of Egyptians, like all the Turks in Egypt, wear the European costume, and at the same time the fez, which is a protest, never lifted, of Oriental independence. Egyptian women, whom we visited in their harems in Helouan, imitate European dress with unfortunately poor success. With this change Egyptians seem to put off the finer aspects of their Eastern culture to make rather bad copies of the West. The lower class retain their Eastern costume: Syrian silk tunics and black cloaks for the men; black robes and veils and brass nose-ornaments for the women. On the desert, black robes over white tunics are frequently seen, floating out almost like wings, which add to that appearance of freedom with which their owners sweep along. But the poorest peasants, who form the mass of the population, wear a straight dark-blue garment. They seem to live, as do the beasts of the field, on the lentils or Egyptian clover, the plants which make the ribbon on each side of the Nile brighter than any green we know. Often we have observed these peasants in some barren village, sitting down beside their cattle or the animals of burden which have carried the food, eating the same plant, leaf and stalk. Camels, laden with the clover look like hay-wagons or moving tree-tops.

Of the other non-European inhabitants of Egypt, the "Copts," whose name was the old Greek word for Egyptians, are those natives, few in number, who have kept that form of the Christian religion which belonged to Egypt before the Mohammedan invasion. They are chiefly clerks or artisans. Theirs is the oldest Christian Church still in existence, and is said to have been founded by St. Mark in Alexandria. Their desert monasteries, built some sixteen hundred years ago have but once in their history been entered by women,— two English scholars who, through a letter to the Patriarch, were recently permitted to search for valuable manuscripts, the pages of which they were allowed to photograph. These ladies found the books decaying, inches deep in dust, and the minds of the monks seemed to be in a similar condition. It is among the followers of this religion that the Western missionaries appear to accomplish most.

The Sais or runners whom we saw chiefly in Cairo are furnished from a distinct tribe of Southern Egyptians.

Hindoos wander through the land as merchants and, true to the psychic quality of their race, as fortune-tellers. Here and there are bronze-faced Nubian servants or vendors of trinkets and shells; but the Nubians are chiefly to be found, as are the proud Bicharines, beyond Luxor, at Assouan, the end of the journey at the First Cataract on the Nubian frontier.

In the midst of the varied types, we ascend day by day toward the source of the river.

Close by the water is always a border of palms; close by the shore is often a line of tall slanting spars. A foot path runs along the edge of the bank some distance above the ebbing river; and along it, out of the Past, come dark-robed figures riding by on camels or on donkeys, or perhaps walking in companies of two or three, absorbed in conversation. Here and there one, solitary, is outlined against the sky.

In the black costumes we saw Egypt in mourning for her desecrated tombs. We came almost to fear some subtle vengeance of contagion, which a romantic writer has suggested; and the keenest impression lingering in our minds is that of the cry which accompanied us along the shore, whether for weal or woe—a shrill, thin, high-pitched, not unmusical cry, coming from a long distance, but filling the atmosphere. Sometimes it was for joy, as on the day of a festival, when we heard it most; sometimes for grief at funerals which crossed the river as of old.

And still the black-robed women are drawing water—Egypt lives again—nay, Egypt has always lived.

Going up the river means sailing deeper and deeper into the heart of a great revelation—where the mountains widen to hold Thebes;—it is going back more than three thousand years to the time of Moses and before, when the greatest temples the world has ever seen, were perfect. One may still read the writing on the walls. It is hearing the other side of a story we have known all our lives,—a side only recently revealed after all these thousands of years.

We have journeyed up this stream to that day when the Euphrates was the river of the East, the Nile, the river of the West, and Israel rose between.

CHAPTER V

From the Love-Story of Egypt

NOW come we to Luxor, the beautiful, the greenest place in the valley,—Luxor, whose tall palms are her living memories of the glory of her great temple-garden. From the days of the Middle Kingdom down to now, the strangers of the world outside have journeyed here to Thebes. She was the "first monumental city of antiquity," where the largest temple of the world still lies upon the sand. Here was its garden, and here the scene of the first historic story of love.

We passed up the stream between what had been the city of the living on the east bank, and the no less splendid city of the dead upon the west. The shore is strewn with the broken shells of the life which has gone, the fragments left here on the sands of time. Finest of all, most beautiful colonnade remaining in Egypt, is the exquisite court of the Temple of Amenhotep III. It is not so large as the great Temple, but fairer and less ruined.

The graceful columns, clusters of papyrus buds, were enclosed by their builders, but today shine down upon the river, and reflected in the water, bring back the spirit of the noble city to us. For

FROM LOVE-STORY OF EGYPT 65

the sunset glow itself lends them its color, while the boats are passing over from the west, as they did in sunsets of old, and the beautiful pillars reveal to us the ancient glory of Thebes.

There is no more Thebes, but ruins; and where the southern suburb lay is the modern Egyptian town of Luxor. There we landed. On the river are a row of curio and picture shops, while the rambling hotels are set far back in fascinating gardens. The air is softer, mellower at Luxor than anywhere in the valley. In the morning, shaking off the dragomen, and with no need for donkey-boys, since the temple is close at hand, we went down among those huge papyrus stems and buds, bathed in light, to dream through a golden day. The silent sunshine gilded the temple floor, the air was fragrant with incense of far-off flowers, birds sang among the columns. We entered into the shadows of the hypostyle hall and rested on the base of a pillar. And we remembered Queen Tia, and thought how the life of Amenhotep III, had expressed itself in beauty—as perhaps no other individual life in the history of the world, has ever been able to do.

For Amenhotep III was king at the height of the golden age of the Empire, the Eighteenth Dynasty. Ahmose of Thebes, the first of his line, had gathered all Egypt to expel her Asiatic usurpers, and with the army behind him and the government in his hand, had re-organized the state. It was a military state,* which, not con-

*Breasted.

tent with securing and developing itself at home, as it had been hitherto, reached out from victory over the alien rulers within itself, to the pursuit of conquest in alien lands. The line began as generals. Amenhotep I followed his father Ahmose. Then came Thutmose I, and the historic family feud of the Thutmosids, with their intense passions raging about Hatshepsut, the Elizabeth of Egyptian history. When she finally rose supreme, and during her long reign of peace and prosperity, her half-brother and husband, Thutmose III, was bound to the priesthood of Amon; but after her death, his long restraint culminated in a series of campaigns so vigorous that he has been called the Napoleon of Egypt, the first world-conqueror. He extended the limits of the Empire as far as they ever were placed; and laid tributary practically the whole of the known world. His son, Amenhotep II, and his grandson, Thutmose IV,—he who uncovered the Sphinx—were each compelled on their accession, to repeat some conquests in Asia, but by the time of Amenhotep III, this was no longer necessary. Not only had the civil power been established by the military within the state, but to the utmost confines of the subject nations, whose rulers as vassals of the Egyptian Pharaoh, were educated at the Egyptian court. In the comfort of Egypt's protection, all individual ambition had been lost.

Safe roads made a fabulous commerce possible, in those fresh days of unexhausted resources. We

THE RIVER AT THEBES

read of trade like that of the Arabian Nights. The customs brought enormous revenues; capital and labor came from the captive nations. All things flowed to the Pharaoh and lifted him to the highest pinnacle. Was ever such wealth, such pride of power?—a pride secure enough to be calm and far above all harshness. He was monarch, not only of Egypt, but from Egypt, of the world. It was not organized society, but organized control, that which the Pyramid expressed, lived out to its largest in the Empire.

As Egypt had been the first nation, so now that other nations had come into being, was she the first world-power. Names that we know begin to appear—though it is not time for Moses for nearly two hundred years. The Court of Babylon acknowledged the authority of Amenhotep over Canaan. The world-conquests of Thutmose, the Napoleon, were followed by the world-politics of his great-grandson Amenhotep. The growth of the world had blossomed into peace.

Egypt's kings had been brother-in-law, nephew, son-in-law or cousin to all the crowned heads of Asia. And not only were the Semitic nations subdued, but they, the conquered, as is always the case, had their effect upon the conquerors. The Semitic influence, strong since prehistoric days, was now moulded into Egypt, producing a new era.

Amenhotep III, after the manner of all early rulers, is supposed to have contracted several alliances with the daughters of other kings; but he showed his supreme power as a Pharaoh, by his ability to assert, in that position, his independence as a man. In his early manhood, perhaps while still crown prince, he made a morganatic marriage purely for love. He proved his greatness above all in that he could raise a lowly-born woman to the highest place in the world. This is the first love-story of history, and now, for the first time in history, is beauty fully revealed.

But the story itself retains the charm of mystery. Despite all search and research, the details are still largely left to our imagination.

Amenhotep issued scarabs to celebrate his marriage, as a ruler might issue medals today. Tia's name and his were carried even unto Greece. Her name is written with his upon all state documents and she now appears with Amenhotep on all public occasions, and is shown to the people beside him on the rich balcony of the palace. This exaltation of the queen was but the summit, at the height of Egypt's glory, of Egypt's reverence for womanhood.

Chateaux and temples had sprung up from end to end of Egypt. In Thebes the magnificent, risen for the second time as capital, and in unprecedented glory, the inhabitants walked in richest costumes of "purple and fine linen."

Amenhotep now became the great patron, fostering the germ of art for the future of the world.

Alone among the temples upon the western

bank of the river, he caused to be built the Palace of Queen Tia, a graceful structure of bricks and wood. It was adorned with brilliant colors. Egypt has always loved her white light broken and defined in the colors of dawn. Color belongs to the objective beginning, it belongs to the "Wings of the Morning;" but the color Egypt loved best was blue, —the highest color, the color of culture, heaven's own color, blue.

Blue were the inner walls of the palace of Tia, blue-tiled with figures in gold-leaf upon them. Had ever a modern queen a more gorgeous or costly abode? The painters put their best work in the palace; and there was not only color but sound, for the soft-toned harp had grown to large dimensions and was combined in an orchestra of four different kinds of instruments, including the Asiatic lyre.*

What the furniture of the palace must have been we can only glean in glimpses of such things which the Egyptians kept safely for the future in the tombs. Many have disappeared. Robbers long ago in Egyptian days, stole them away to perish. But it is only a short time since Mr. Davis, a man from the newest and farthest west of nations, working here at this ancient capital, came upon the tomb of Queen Tia's unknown parents. No Egyptologist can enter the opening to such a

*Breasted.
I believe the palace of Amenhotep III has been one of the three sites in Egypt excavated for the Metropolitan Musuem in New York, which now contains one of its beautiful ceilings.

place without a feeling of awe, and at the same time of expectant exultation, since it is for him the way back into the ancient Empire. The robbers had been there before, but something had frightened them away, and they had dropped their booty in the tomb passage, where Mr. Davis found it:—a chariot of fine workmanship with an historic battle-relief; a chair which, the Empress Eugénie declareed, was like those of the Empire in France; and back in the tomb-chamber a canopied bier, upon which lay Tia's parents side by side.

In Cairo, and in the museums of the world where the spoils which the nations have taken from Egypt are hoarded, are fragments of tapestries equal to the best work of Europe, which once adorned the walls of such a palace; chairs and ottomans such as we use today; tables, draught-boards of ebony and ivory, with fine inlaying; vessels of gold and silver, in heaviest and yet most chaste and exquisite workmanship; crystal, and glass, so beautifully colored that the world has never yet re-learned the art of making it.

Before the palace of Tia, Amenhotep caused a lake to be excavated for her, the supposed embankments of which may still be seen. From the dawn of history this people had known how to conserve and manipulate the water-supply upon which their life as a people depended. Just as all public works, especially breaking ground for a canal, were always inaugurated by the king with great ceremony, so, when this excavation was

FROM LOVE-STORY OF EGYPT 71

ready, Amenhotep himself opened the gates to let in the water, on the day which celebrated for the twelfth time his coronation. He and the queen sailed out over the lake, and a gorgeous festival was made of the occasion.*

So, near to its lake, is conjured up before our imagination the palace of Amenhotep's Queen Tia, a veritable fairy-palace, because existing only in our dream. But even a fragment of its floor-painting, may give a suggestion of all that must have been—a fragment the feet of this beloved, vanished queen have pressed. It represents three ducks among the lotus, which, with the papyrus, were the first national flowers. And it unfolds the fact that the artists who adorned this palace were skilled in catching the most fleeting, transitory moment which marks motion, and therefore reveals life.

The palace of Queen Tia is gone, it belonged to the fleeting, earth-life phase of the individual,—brilliant, beautiful and frail. The temples were permanent, for the everlasting god and the memorial of the king, such as men seek to make their temples today.

It was the temple which concentrated and expressed all the beauty of the age at Amenhotep's will. The work of Egypt was building—we cannot wonder at the development of the task-master. The wise men of Egypt were her architects—it is they who above all were the counsellors of her

*Breasted

kings, they, whose writings were preserved as proverbs; they, of whom several, after a millenium had passed since they slept, were worshipped as gods in their country. So did it happen a thousand years later to the chief architect of Amenhotep III, who bore the king's own name and wrought the king's wish in stone.

A great era of building had set in and it seems as if Amenhotep, out of the fullness of joy in his own heart, had said to his architects and artists:

"You are given men, material, and the conventional forms, what new life will you create?"

And they did create two new things for the future of the world.* One was that small but exquisite cella temple, in which the holy of holies is set within a colonnade, the columns guarding it on all sides. Do we not discover in this a prenatal influence upon Greece?

The other development grew out of the old arrangement, the tabernacle form, and took shape in this Temple of Luxor, where we have been all the morning. It is found not only in the temples which followed this in Egypt—but many a time when we have looked upon a cathedral of Europe we have unknowingly beheld something made possible by that which originated here.

Temples were rising at the bidding of Amenhotep in Egypt, Nubia and Sinai. The state temple of Amon, now Karnak, in Thebes, which had been

*The following description of the temples is based upon the account of the temple development in Breasted's "History of Egypt.

added to successively by Amenhotep's ancestors, was enlarged and fabulously enriched by him; a new pylon added, stelae made of lapis lazuli, floors and walls encrusted with silver and gold and precious stones—the whole a gorgeous mass of color, its shining obelisks pointing to the sky. That temple, lifeless today, with its dark mysteries, must then have been a reservoir of light, its glittering walls and towers giving forth the radiance of the Sun-god. And before it, in the radiance, stood the calm colossal figure of the king, looking across the river, where lay the palace of his Heart's Desire.

At Karnak too, Amenhotep built the temple to Mut, the mother-goddess, his sacred ideal of motherhood, in whose character the queen appears; and there he dug her sacred lake, as he had the pleasure lake for Tia. As the temple of Amon at Karnak was built to a glorified idea of manhood, which Amenhotep represented in himself; so the Temple of Mut was built to the idea of womanhood, whose crown queen Tia wore. Having connected the sanctuaries of Amon and Mut, Amenhotep made a wondrous avenue of sphinxes, which extends for a mile and a half to Luxor, uniting the temple he was building there in one harmonious scheme with Karnak. Between the two he laid out a vast garden.

For at Luxor, the Theban suburb, Amenhotep had found a small temple to the state-god Amon. He pulled it down. The Egyptians themselves often pulled down to rebuild. Then his architects constructed this great temple, not, like the Karnak building, added to and enlarged about a small central beginning, but on one simple, perfect plan. Behind this hypostyle where we have rested is the holy of holies. Its carvings have since been plastered over, for it has been used as a Coptic Church. An altar, perhaps Roman, stands before it in the hypostyle itself. The chambers around the sanctuary have become so ruined as to lose their cloistered look, while their mystery is strangely enhanced by their appearance as a maze. One obtains some idea of the intricate ground-plan. A small side-chamber, which opens toward the outer corridor, and faces the eastern girdle-wall still standing, is the birth chapel on the walls of which is the birth-story of Amenhotep, the son of Amon, whose name means "Amon rests."

Before the hypostyle hall, the majestic court grew into being, with its double colonnade of papyrus-bud columns. It completed the temple except for a pylon before it. Then Amenhotep or his architect dreamed a dream, which men still embody in the architecture of today. Before the court it was planned to erect a second hypostyle hall, on an altogether grander scale than had ever been attempted before. It was probably intended to place before this hall another court, where the somewhat rude forecourt of Rameses II stands today. The hall was to have a central aisle or nave between two rows of seven giant columns with flower capitals. The rows of columns on each side of these would be much lower, and the hall would be lighted by openings in the story of wall which joined the lower and higher roof. Thus did the basilica and the cathedral form originate!

Amenhotep passed away before more than the twice seven great columns were standing. His son, for reasons we shall come to understand, was obliged to abandon the grand hall just taking shape. The drums of the other columns were later used to enclose the lonely nave. Rameses II patched it out with his huge forecourt and pylon, his obelisks and colossal statues.

A detail, small but significant, lingers in our minds. In the Temple of Luxor, through the pylon of Rameses II, where a corner of his forecourt is unexcavated, a little white mosque clings like a bird's nest among the capitals of the giant pillars. In the earth beneath it, rests the body of a Mohammedan saint, and to excavate would be to disinter. Hence the columns are hidden and— preserved.

In another corner of this court, behind the figure of Rameses, is a treasure picture, a relief which is for us a restoration of the temple. A festival procession of the priests with Rameses' sons approaches the great pylon, before which are the collossi of the king, with the two obelisks—one of which is now in the Place de la Concorde in Paris. Flags are flying from the tall poles before the pylon, and reminded us somehow of the king's birthday before St. Mark's.

But the court of Amenhotep III remains alone to us for beauty and the giant nave beyond, alone for a great thought. The idea was carried out to its perfection by Seti I, and Rameses II, in the hypostyle at Karnak, the largest hall in the world. But the unfinished hall of Luxor, eloquent of many things in its broken incompleteness, gave the suggestion for the later sacred architecture.

Amenhotep reared one more glorious building, his mortuary temple, which, like those of his fathers, rose on the western plain. In it was expressed the summit of his prosperity; and from all that we can learn of it, it was probably the most exquisite work of art that Egypt ever saw. We can dream of the sculptures which adorned it, of the avenue of jackals which led up to the two collosi before it. The thirty foot high stela which marked the "Station of the King," where he stood to perform the ritual, was incased in precious metal and studded with jewels. Another, of lapis lazuli, recorded all that Amenhotep, the king, had done for his father Amon. How could the king fear dying, to enter into such immortal glory, and be worshipped as a god!

But this temple was too perfect to escape destruction, that its material might be used by a later ruler, who was the Pharaoh of the Exodus,—too perfect to have lasted, lest it discourage the future. Only a trace remains; Luxor is still the best we know in Egypt.

The great stela of the mortuary temple lies

FROM LOVE-STORY OF EGYPT

broken and denuded on the western plain. Out of nature, back to nature, have passed the beautiful forms. The avenue of jackals, which led up to the temple, is a winding path through the fields to the colossi. They alone, after repeated damages from which they have been recovered, still hold themselves above the encroachments of Time. Strangely enough, one of these inarticulate stone statues found a voice to speak itself in music. Whether a crack filled with dew, vibrated when the sun's rays touched it, can only be surmised; but for centuries the broken figure, turned as it is toward the East, greeted the dawn with music. Distinguished visitors travelled from Greece to hear it and left their names upon the base. The voice ceased with the statue's restoration.

The faces of these figures have smoothed themselves out to an inscrutable expression, while the wisdom of the centuries was being gathered. But there exist rare portraits of this king. The work of the sculptors in the temples has lived longer than that of the painters in the palaces. Even that color, with which the statues and reliefs were clothed has dropped away from them. But we can see how the masters of the plastic art succeeded not only in catching a representative moment in a general type of life, but in seizing and holding as never before, the idea in an individual, the mood of a man.

In the British Museum, far away in London, is a face of this first lover in history, the royal Amenhotep, which shows the power of the sculptors of his day to catch the soul of the man. DeQuincy said of it that it unites "the expressions of ineffable benignity with infinite endurance."

The king was gathered to his fathers in the rough mountain valley. Later Queen Tia, the Beloved, died and was buried.

During a recent winter, Prof. Petrie, excavating in the remote desert of Sinai, found there in a temple a portrait head of Tia. Hitherto her face had only been imagined from a few unsatisfactory reliefs, which were necessarily profiles; and the identity of which was not certain. This little head belonged to a statuette, the whole of which had been no more than one foot high. The head was all that remained. Yet Prof. Petrie considered this one treasure, alone worth the whole year's work. It seems to prove that another face, carved in marble, which he calls "the supreme queen's head" was also a portrait of this queen who inspired such devotion in the heart of the most glorious king of Egypt. The small head lately found is, Petrie tells us, evidently taken from life with great freedom and great delicacy, especially about and under the eyes. Describing it he speaks of the "haughty dignity" of the face, blended with "fascinating directness and personal appeal;" of the lips drawn down with disdain yet free from malice, lips full yet delicate.

The queen's crown rests upon the haughty little head. At the time of the discovery, it furnished the best description we had of such a head-dress, which had been known only from drawings of its folded vulture wings.* The real gold crown was still hidden away with the queen. This sculptured one appeared to represent gold open-work, with the queen's name above the brow between the two serpents signifying power, and the two wings of protection.

But a greater discovery has since been made. Mr. Theo. M. Davis has found the tomb of the queen herself. It had been unmolested except by a visit from the priestly enemies of her noble son. They erased his name wherever found, without carrying away the gold or harming the queen's body, except to turn it over. The tomb is remarkable for several things, including this priestly visit; for its immunity from robbery, and for its treasures, consequently intact. Among these is the little figure of a water-girl, done with such freedom, that if discovered anywhere else it would be imputed to Greece rather than to conventional Egypt. But the time of Tia's son, during which she was interred, was the one reign when Egyptian art broke all the bonds of tradition. The queen's gold crown was found with her, the first crown of a queen to be discovered. It is the sacred head-dress, indicating that the god protects the royal person as the vulture protects her young. The vulture is the emblem of motherhood and is sacred to Mut, the Great Mother. Hence the mother-

*Such as Cleopatra's at Dendera.

queens, protected and protecting, wore vulture head-dresses.

The queen's body seemed perfect and yet escaped from her discoverers. There is that in Egypt which is not tangible, which cannot be transported. It was there in the steps of the workmen at Sakkara—the actual footprints of a vanished life—just as it passed. There are many things one sees, many things one does not see—things which are glimpsed or guessed. Through this dark rock chamber, a tiny stream of water had found its way while the queen had slept for thirty-five hundred years; and when the light was let in and they touched her, she vanished—there was only a handful of dust. So she eluded them, so she escaped the gaze of irreverent tourists.

Amenhotep III and Queen Tia are gone, but the importance of their love marriage was not fully revealed until after the old king's death, in their son.

In the last days of Amenhotep's reign, a subtle change had taken place in the condition of the Empire, scarcely seen and not understood by him. Luxury had overbalanced itself in the lives of the people, with their elaborate homes and costumes, —their wigs, their pointed sandals, all their affectations—the extreme of their civilization.

On the other hand while the kings of Egypt had represented divinity to the nation, the people knew Amenhotep as a man. He was a mighty hunter. With no more enemies to conquer, there was no

OUT OF THE PAST CAME FIGURES

FROM LOVE-STORY OF EGYPT

conquest left but of the wild bulls in the marshes, the lions in the hills. Amenhotep several times celebrated his accomplishments in this direction by an issue of scarabs. But no king before him had become thus familiar to his people. He made himself less than a god in his anxiety to record his human achievements. His divinity is expressed on the human side—especially in his marriage and in his relation with foreign powers. He is no more a god, ruling over a valley which is the world and holding it for the god whom he succeeds; but a king who, ruling over other rulers, is a human brother to them. Yet his extended authority also suggests the larger idea of a universal god. Church and state are one. The state is the expression of its god's authority.

In the days of Amenhotep, the priesthoods were seeking, each in its own local worship, the god who was to be worthy the Empire and to rule the world. Imperialism was about to express itself in thought—and dissolve. This was the dawn of philosophy. In the meantime the Empire was already breaking on its edges. And Amenhotep was lulled to sleep in his dream of beauty.

Amenhotep IV, the son of the first historic love-marriage, the marriage of Amenhotep III and Queen Tia, is the first idealist, the first to stand out alone in matters of the deepest consciousness, the first to claim a religious revelation—Breasted calls him the first individual in history.

Though he gained his conception through Re,

Amenhotep IV saw that none of the old gods would satisfy it. They were limited by defining personalities. His idea was even more abstract than the monotheisms which followed it. "Before science was, he had thought out an entirely scientific system."* The sun's disk or "aton" represented the heat in all life. Thus Amenhotep IV obtained the idea of one source and one power, as it is manifested through the sun.

The Aton was never figured with any form of man or beast—from the sun's disk proceeded innumerable rays ending in hands which brought life and power to all things on the earth. As opposed to the figures of the gods, it was a symbol which spoke a universal word, not to be misunderstood, even by alien peoples. The gods had needed interpreters. Dauntless in his convictions against the world upon which he stood, the young king was always deeply influenced by his mother, and by his probably Semitic wife who is always portrayed with him. He built a temple to his god in the garden between Karnak and Luxor. But his new worship quickly came into conflict with the established priesthoods, especially with the priesthood of Amon-Re, the former state-god, whom he had deposed. So bitter and violent was this conflict that when it was over, neither priesthood nor king was left in Thebes. The halls of Karnak and Luxor were deserted, the priests scattered, the very name of Amon was chiseled out wherever it occur-

*Petrie

red, though that place were in the name of the king's father, on his father's sculptured form. And the king's own name was changed. He is no longer Amenhotep IV, but emerges from the tempest, as Ikhnaton, the individual who is the "Glory of the Aton."

Life must always be expressing itself in form, but where the form crystallizes to prevent growth, life must always break through or transform it. This son of Amenhotep III, worthily developing on a higher plane, the ideal nature which in his father found expression in the beauty of these Theban halls, was obliged by that very nature to overthrow and desert these scarce finished halls of his father and even his father's name. His spirit had leaped into being, destroying the forms which held it. But overcome by the bitterness of the struggle, he left Thebes for his new capital Akhetaton, where is now the Egyptian Tell-el-Amarna, which we passed further down the river.

Here he held his court and established the worship of the Aton. Thus the marriage of Amenhotep III, and Tia, proved portentous; for their son Ikhnaton, dwelling in the ideal as more real and lasting than the material, became the heretic king of Egyptian history, the reformer, worshipping the "one God of Light in the form of the Sun-disk."

There were no figures of gods in the temples of Ikhnaton's new capital at Akhetaton—nothing but the Sun. In Egypt the figures of Amon were destroyed; and Egyptian art, though only for a reign, was set free from the conventional symbols.

But the people were not developed to this high conception, the heart of the country was torn, the Empire fell apart, and a few reigns later the dynasty itself passed out.

It was the natural course of events.

While Ikhnaton was establishing the new religion and working out the thought of the one source of life, there came to him letters from his vassals in Asia begging him for aid. There were disaffections, invasions. A new generation had forgotten the army of Egypt and the might of Egypt's king. But either the king did not understand, or he understood too well; for the Hittite power had arisen in the north and waxed treacherous and strong.

An army was needed to preserve the Empire form; but Ikhnaton did not lead his army into Asia. Perhaps it was not so much that the provinces were of less value to him in their essential life, than was his ideal, in which all life was one; but that the holding of them by Egypt was less vital to him. Ikhnaton's course of inaction must have seemed utterly impractical from any contemporary material point of view, as it does to some historians today; impractical for the good of Egypt and the arbitrary organization of the Empire.

The height and breadth of an abstract conception had been reached by Ikhnaton alone. The national feeling and the national god still meant to Egypt the uniting of a certain number of men against others. It was true of them as of other nations that the form of god they worshipped expressed their genius; were they not symbolically right in believing that it was their god who triumphed or was conquered?

When the Empire had become a world power, suggesting and revealing a universal god, Ikhnaton had seen that this god must be in all—therefore he, the king, could no longer fight to hold the Empire. His god was not, like the idea of Amon, a "God of battles," but the god whose life was in all. The bravery of his race turned not in him to conquest of a foreign people, but to facing his own with his ideal.

Ikhnaton and his immediate successors lost the Empire in Asia, which was never entirely regained; but in reading history we must perceive each fact, not with regard to an individual or a nation, but with regard to its place in the whole development of mankind. Something greater than the individual, greater than the good of any one country, was moving through Egypt.

Life was probably not destroyed in the provinces, any more than the Egyptian army would have destroyed it. They had to learn to struggle for themselves and some developed a growth of their own. The form of a state religion had for once been broken through, the form of a state now fell apart and permitted other lands to rise.

In Ikhnaton was the consummation, the flaming up of the religious life of Egypt.

When the state religion of Amon was restored with the new dynasty, it was only as a form, from which the spiritual life was gone, the religious form, which instead of being expressed in the state, had begun to absorb the state, until the state came to assume the form.

Neither was the city of Thebes ever the same after Ikhnaton, not even in the days of that great builder, Rameses II.

Akhetaton has vanished. Tell-el-Amarna is today the desert place of the Abstraction. The city which once expressed this thought and lay there upon the desert, has passed, a flower as spiritual as the dew-flower, whose life is drawn up in the glare of day. There only remain the collection of letters, the most remarkable, because the earliest collection of letters in the world. They tell the story from without.

Not in any weakness of Amenhotep, as Breasted thinks it was—, or of his son, but in the evanescent growing quality of conditions, was the change that came after Amenhotep's reign. His was the perfect flowering, that was all. Out of it arose the idealism of Ikhnaton, and the breaking of the bonds of the old form, even to the limits of the Empire organization—a consequence neither father nor son could themselves have fully foreseen.

Yet thus was the way prepared for Israel.

More imposing than the colossal statues of

Amenhotep III, or Rameses II, is the spiritual figure of the son of Amenhotep III and the Queen Tia, Ikhnaton, the idealist, the "Glory of the Light."

CHAPTER VI

Before the Temple

KARNAK, Temple of Temples, "National Sanctuary," "Throne of the World," lying so vast, so broken, so open to the sunlight, where thou hast yielded up the secret of Egypt and her history,—how may one tell of thee!

When the evening and the morning were the second day, we went by the old way to Karnak. It is Amenhotep's avenue of sphinxes that leads thence from the Luxor temple. At first the small bazaars of the native Egyptian village cling about the road, but it leads off into the palms where was the ancient garden and where, here and there, hamlets of mud huts seek to hide themselves. All the way, the broken sphinxes, one by one take up and carry on the story of the grand processions that passed between the temples—especially at Amon's Feast of Opet, which for importance was as the Hebrew Passover at Jerusalem, or the Christian Easter of today at Rome. More than once, and once on this very road, great changes of government were accomplished at this festival.

For a mile and a half we rode northward until we drew near to the home of the state religion of

Egypt. Passing a ruined group of buildings to the east—the Temple of Mut, which Amenhotep reared to the goddess of the Theban triad,—we reach a meeting of the ways. An avenue of sphinxes leads at right angles eastward to the northern entrance of the Mother-goddess' temple, from whence another avenue, parallel with our own, stretches to the first of many gateways approaching the side of the Temple of Amon. We keep on our way, and just ahead, there stands one of the most beautiful doors in all Egypt, a late portal to the Temple of Khonsu, the son of Amon and Mut. We dismount and enter, that we may climb the pylon for our first survey of Karnak, the Great.

Beyond the court at our feet we catch a glimpse of dark and empty halls, where now the sun lies flecked upon the floor. This little Temple of Khonsu has its own interest, its contribution to the dramatic story of the state, but we are not ready for that now. From the solemn and mysterious chambers below us we lift our eyes to look across the billowy sands. What mighty wreck, like a great ship, lies there? More than a thousand feet in length we trace its shape. The pylons at the front are high, the great hall with its broken windows, rises in the midst, but the low sides at either end of the whole structure are all but washed over by the sand. In the submergence the height of the hall itself is not realized from without. The waves are up to the top of Rameses III's chapel, and in places surge over the walls. In the first space, a single rounded column holds itself erect, and near the middle of the length are several shafts still standing—the others have gone over.

It was in Karnak that the ship of state went down.

For in Karnak the whole state was gathered up.

Since the first historic day, when Menes, the first king of a united Egypt, appears upon earth's stage as "Horus," the successor of the god who ruled the land—from that day even unto this, the unity of church and state has been an accomplished fact. It has sprung from a fundamental perception, over which has developed a great division. For men felt truly in the beginning that power was divine, and that the laws of Man should express the Sacred Will. But they limited God by forms, each man after his kind; and with that sense of unity which also came by intuition, each has attempted to extend his finite idea of God and God's Will over the rest of mankind. Hence have arisen the bitterest struggles of history, and the separations of church and state. Yet, fundamentally, they cannot be separated. The latest and freest of nations had its beginnings partly for worship—a free worship.

In early Egyptian days, among many others, there was Ptah, the Builder in Memphis; Re in Heliopolis; Amon in Thebes. When the land was united all these forms existed together. The Egyptians built them temples of stone, and made them rituals of worship. Through those centuries of the longest history any people have ever known, beginning with the beginning, they added to the temples and elaborated the rituals—till every figure on the temple walls was prescribed in all its proportions, which had their mystical significance.

The chief business of Egypt was building. The first genius was wrought into stone. For men dreamed how long their work would have to last. They must make the form to contain the god that it might also suggest him. Egypt became the land of temples. Strangely like and yet unlike, the building of the national temple at Thebes, is the building of the national temple at Jerusalem. Strangely like the same story also, reads the record of the offerings to the Christian Church of St. Mark. Greece also had her Parthenon. It is only in our own day that the making of great public buildings has superseded to some extent the building of the temple which has been the chief business of all ages.

In time, in Egypt, the form became all. The glory of the gods destroyed the land. The wealth, constantly drawn in large endowments from the state, overtopped the economic balance, the priestly power dethroned the king.

We descend to the darkened mysteries of this little temple of Khonsu to think over the story, before going on to Karnak.

In the Egyptian Middle Ages the rise of a Theban family to power had made Thebes the capital.

With the development of the Empire, Amon, the god of Thebes, became the state god—combined with Re of Heliopolis as Amon-Re. The Egyptian official worship was always Sun-worship, whether of Amon, Re, or Aton. The temples were the shadows of the Sun.

The Temple of Amon at Karnak became the national temple of the state religion, added to by king after king of the Empire. These kings wrote their conquests on its outer walls, their offerings within. It is the book of their history. Karnak, more than anything else, represents what Egypt stood for—the building of the temple.

From the time of Thutmose III, it became the chief glory of each king to outdo his predecessors in gifts to the state god. As their wealth increased, the power of the priests by which they could control the king increased, and the more they could command. It was all out of proportion, out of harmony, we can see now that the break was sure to come. But how many individuals in any age can understand the tendencies which are working through themselves? An economic evil once set going, interacts with conditions and grows constantly greater until it destroys itself. Each king for his own glory and later for the preservation of his position, added to the power of the priests. And the priesthood of Amon received many times more than all the rest. It therefore gained control of the others.

Only once while the temple was building and

while the priests were fettering the kings,—only once, as we have seen, was the form broken through by the life within. That was the first religious revolution in history. And after that there was no more life in the form. The story of the state temple is a study in organization.

In the Eighteenth Dynasty the priesthoods of Egypt, each with its orders of rank, had become united, with the High Priest of Amon as their head. He was chief ecclesiastic, head of an hierarchy whose control reached every corner of the land. Thebes, the state capital, became the religious capital. In the Theban Temple the records of all the priesthoods were kept.

In the Nineteenth Dynasty the High Priest of Amon had succeeded in making his office hereditary. The Pharaoh was still, as always in theory, the head of the worship of Egypt for all the people. When the days of conquest were over, the chief use of the Pharaoh in the hands of the priests, was to minister to the Temple. The Temple had laid hold of the temporal power.

The gold country of Nubia was given to the state god in the Nineteenth Dynasty. At first the Viceroy of Nubia was Governor of the Gold Country of Amon. By the latter part of the Twentieth Dynasty the High Priest of Amon was Viceroy of Nubia.

It is in the days after the glory of the Empire that we trace the history, not of religious feeling, but of the binding and destroying influence of conventional forms.

Feast days were added to the already elaborate religious calendar, and while these days called for more revenue, as holidays they depleted labor, the source of revenue.

The people wrought in heaviness to support the burden; Rameses III, of the Twentieth Dynasty, was forced to depend upon mercenary troops and his treasury went bare. It was a state, bankrupted by its religious order. The poor man's god unfortunately lived in a palace.

Yet the priests did a good work. Theirs were the only schools and universities. They were the conservers of learning, the preservers of the old language.

The hereditary head of the priesthood of Egypt, entrenched in the eternal palace of the god, with boundless wealth at his command, watched the last struggle of the kingship. The princely priest, Amenhotep, married Isis, the daughter of Rameses VI. A little older than the last three brothers of that king, this Amenhotep became their tutor.

One more concession he compelled from Rameses IX, the last of all. The Temple under the hereditary priesthood might collect its own revenues. It thus became a separate state.

The time was ready. Amenhotep, the High Priest, had a son, Hrihor, who was also the son of the daughter of Rameses VI, and who became High Priest. And then, the change was effected —quite naturally, it seems,—when one puts together the findings of several Egyptologists. The last of the family of Rameses slips somehow into desuetude, and the priest, with all proper forms and ceremonies, stands in his place. The carvings in this temple of Khonsu tell the story without words. And the records of the time reveal, with the ascent of Hrihor, the absolute sway of magical forms. It was a state established on and ruled by the constant violation of law, in perversion of the truth.

But Hrihor was unable to extend his temporal control over all Egypt. The increasing power of his father and himself, had long meant the increasing weakness and the final dissolution of the state. A new kingship had arisen in the north out of that weakness, to block his way; and to cut off Thebes, the religious capital, from the circulation of the world.

As High Priest of Amon, Hrihor had still a measure of power over all Egypt. Nesubenebded, the Delta King, passed the High Priest's envoy on to Syria for cedar of Lebanon for Amon's sacred barge, when he would not have done the same at the behest of the Pharaoh Rameses.*

Hrihor, as king, was unable to control Nesubenebded. From this time on the kingdom was broken, Thebes remaining an ecclesiastical state independent and untaxed. Seldom able to control the country, refusing to be controlled, it usually succeeded in breaking the country. By an old method, the difficulty was solved for the moment.

*See the story of the diplomatic messenger in Breasted's History of Egypt.

A grandson of Hrihor, Paynozim at Thebes, married a grand-daughter of Nesubenebded. It is recorded how she came south for her marriage. Poor, sweet Maat-ka-ra, of the beautiful portrait and the elaborate coffin—one of the finest discovered in Thebes,—proving the love and regret that went with her down into the tomb. She died, still young and fair, in childbirth,—and lies now with the little one in the museum at Cairo, a tragedy of long ago.

With the accession of the High Priest to the throne, the high priesthood ceased to be a separately hereditary office. King after king, of the Twenty-first and Twenty-second Dynasties, in trying to control the Temple as well as the state, added to the priestly revenue, but placed a son of his own, usually not the crown prince, in the High Priest's position. Then it was brother against brother, the strong house divided against itself, while the High Priests, one after another, again sought to found a separate line.

The long story was drawing to a close.

The Egypt of the Twenty-second Dynasty was a feudal state.

Under the next, the nation went utterly to pieces, back to the small component parts which preceded the two kingdoms in pre-historic days.

Outside, the possessions in Asia were long gone. In spite of reminiscences of Egypt's power, which always caused an Egyptian party in Israel, Egypt had in reality become the derision of the petty

THE FAMILY IN EGYPT

states she once so freely chastised. And even while the city kings of the Delta struggled with one another within Egypt, they looked fearfully over the border and beheld the new Empire of Assyria arising in the East—gaining power as Egypt declined, consolidating as Egypt disintegrated. Already those border states which had once constituted Egypt's Empire, now made the Empire of Assyria. All that the Delta rulers, each with his individual instinct of self-preservation, could do, backed by the former greatness of Egypt, was to stir up revolt against the new authority in those states that lay between.

But while the petty princes of Egypt wrestled with one another and watched the East, a darkness came up from the south. Their first conqueror was of their own making, though possibly they knew it not. The foundations were laid in the struggles of the previous dynasty with the priesthood of Thebes. In the gradual destruction of the state, the priesthood had pulled down the house about its own head.

But Nubia, long Egyptianized by Egyptian colonists and customs, long held by Amon and never lost as the Asiatic provinces had been,— Nubia, the farthest, the last to be disturbed by internal disaster, was the last refuge of the god. Thebes was between it and the power which was in the north. At some time in the Twenty-second Dynasty there had been a flight into Nubia of the priests. In the Twenty-third Dynasty Egypt became aware of a new state, with its capital Napata, far up at the 4th Cataract. Amon was its god and it was elaborately organized as a sacerdotal state, possessing all which Egypt had ever known. So mysterious its origin and remote its position, that the later Greeks, fascinated by the romance of its existence and its culture, looked back upon it as the source of civilization in Egypt, and therefore in the world. Nevertheless, we known now the true story of Ethiopia.

About 720 B. C. Piankhi, a king of this kingdom of Ethiopia, marched forth to the temporary conquest of Egypt. He used the Delta kings against one another as later, in Europe, Philip Augustus used Richard and John. The Twenty-fifth Dynasty were Ethiopians: Shabaka, who established Piankhi's line in Egypt, and Taharka, whose name we know in Hebrew story. The petty principalities into which Egypt had been broken, became vassal states of Nubia. The political power of the Theban High Priest of Amon was gone. But the new kings kept the Pharaonic titles and revered the gods of Egypt. They built on the Karnak temple at Thebes and they moved to the north and even dreamed of recovering the lost Empire.

As a beginning and in order to at least protect their country from that threatening danger which was lowering in the East, they attempted another stirring up of the kingdoms in Palestine and Syria. Assyria appeared on their horizon and dealt deadly punishment. Several times was Egypt saved,

once by the pestilence which destroyed a host of
the Assyrian army and delivered Jerusalem, as
Isaiah had promised Hezekiah; again by a revived
strength in Egypt. The third time, Memphis fell,
and Taharka fled southward—only to be reinstated by princes and priests as soon as the Assyrian
had departed. On the commemorative stela of
Esarhaddon the tables are reversed: Assyria looms
large—and Egypt is a captive dwarf.

Seven times in all did an Assyrian knock at the
gate of Egypt. Three times he crossed the threshold. The last time the Assyrian army, under
Ashurbanipal, marched up the long valley and
sacked Thebes, carrying away, as they had in
Jerusalem, the gold and silver of the temple, the
wealth, long held safely in the inviolate temple
fortresses, after Egypt, swept with the winds of
conflict, had become a desert.

Thebes, the religious city, whose glory had been
as the morning, a material glory such as no city
of the earth had ever displayed, was now darkened
and desolated, her very memories desecrated.

In early conquests, it was always the temple
which was destroyed, as it was a people's god who
had fallen—the form which their genius gave to
that which was within them. Nothing could so
well represent the conquest of their spirit. We
recall the probably necessary destruction of the
Mahdi's tomb in the Soudan within our own days.

At the close of Egyptian history there was a
brief revival imposed by a Libyan with the aid of

Greek mercenaries. To this time belongs the Pharaoh Hophra of Hebrew Scripture. In Egypt the sunset went back to the dawn which had been, before ever Amon rose supreme. Then came the night of eclipse, with the long and unbroken series of conquests by Persians, Greeks, Romans, Mohammedans, French and English. Conqueror after conqueror has swept over the land, foreigner after foreigner holding it until today.

This then, is the story of Egypt's national religious organization—the end with the beginning—a study typical of organization for all time. It is form, not in the material world, but in the realm of mind. We realize that the image may exist even as an idea.

It will be necessary when we come to enter the Temple of Egypt, to begin with the outmost and latest building, and work back to the time of Egypt's glory. We shall know these kings and the part each took in the building of the Temple, shall know them in the House of Amon, with their work and their records there. From one to another they will pass us back to the centre of the golden age. So we would know beforehand from the end of the story, the true inner significance of the Temple, and then forgetting the later details, dwell on its perfection, realizing what it represented and gave us,—in contrast with something else which arose in and came out of Egypt.

All this as one would overlook Karnak—still only partly excavated. Thou Temple of Temples, not only of Egypt, but of the world, standing for the outer form which clothes religion, but empty of religion now, thou hast thy message too.

CHAPTER VII

The House of Amon

HAVING thus been initiated in the little temple of Khonsu, having, as it were, prepared ourselves in the ante-chamber, we passed out of the gate and turned once more toward the fallen form which above all things in Egypt, represents the fallen state. Not even the remounting of resisting donkeys and the roughness of our pilgrimage could make us forget that we were now to enter The Temple of Egypt itself.

Our way leads over the billowy sands by the south side of the structure. Presently, descending a hill, we come round to the front of the great pylon, where broken bits of sculpture, recently excavated, can no more than indicate a once splendid avenue. Since Amenhotep's time, it has led from the portal of Karnak, ever advancing to encroach upon it, westward to the Nile. This pylon, the largest in Egypt, belongs to the Ptolemaic period. Though Karnak is in ruins, it is not yet complete. The old scaffolding of the workmen clings to the giant towers, and marks above all else, the desertion and desolation of the temple.

This gateway was the final seal to the work of

THE HOUSE OF AMON

Rameses II, by those appreciative foreign rulers who did so much to emphasize Egypt and who were impartial to all her gods, in whom they found their own. Rameses' great hypostyle hall properly presupposed a court and a final pylon before it. The temple plan, as we have seen, was always practically the same: first and outmost the pylon, then the outer court with the altar, then the hypostyle hall and vestibules beyond, and lastly, the holy of holies, surrounded by a corridor and chambers. But if, in an attempt to outdo former efforts, a larger hypostyle hall was added before the pylon, it would again be preceded by a court, and an outer pylon in proportion. This series, ever increasing in size, was twice added to Karnak, not to mention the addition of Thutmose III at the other end.

As we stand between the modern iron railings in the huge open portal, from which the ancient gates are long gone, across the court and far beyond, door after door shows in diminishing perspective. It should be so in a straight line to the inner sanctuary. Karnak itself is a "Book of the Portals," each once the outmost, and all inscribed. On the south side a similar line, almost at right angles, leads up to the central court. They suggest the stages of the mystery. It is a temple behind a temple. What must it have been when all the doors were closed!

When we crossed the threshold, we were fortunate enough to be alone, and we found within the court, the largest temple-court in the world, a vast sunny silence. The pylon before us was a double mountain of stone, except in the centre, where the masonry was propped with cross supports which interfered with our vista. Heaps of débris tell the chapters not written otherwise. Out of it all, near the centre, blooms one great flower, a single rounded shaft, lifting a lotus capital. Taharka of Ethiopia, who fought Sennacherib on the side of Israel, at the time that Hezekiah spread the Assyrian's letter in the Temple at Jerusalem—he it was who reared the lonely lily. It was not lonely then. For some reason which has perished with the structure, Taharka raised in this foremost court, a building of twelve such lotus-pillars, each as large as Trajan's column. This one remains to tell what the others were.

The court was placed in front of Rameses' giant hypostyle hall by the so-called Bubastide Pharaohs of the Twenty-second Dynasty. The origin of Sheshonk, founder of the line, who married the last daughter of the Theban-Tanite house, descended from Paynozim and Maatkara, is a matter of dispute. He would seem not to have been a Libyan, as some scholars suppose, for his name, and that of his successors indicates an Eastern origin. Was he, the first Sheshonk, "the man of Susa," as Petrie suggests, a Babylonian or Persian adventurer at the court and in the service of the king? If so, his marriage with the princess Karamat, of the priestly Twenty-first Dynasty, must be one of the lost romances of early days.

THE HOUSE OF AMON 105

Thus again the royal line was carried through the crown princess, whose name, as it appears, handed down in all its variations through this Dynasty, is a corruption of Maat-ka-ra, the name of the Tanite princess, her ancestress, who came to Thebes, and the prenomen of the great Hatshepsut. Like those queens, she has the double cartouche of the royal ruler in her own right.

We have seen how each founder of a new dynasty brought fresh strength to the contest with the internal conditions of Egypt, and for a moment rallied her and held back her decline, till the strength of the line had diminished, when the same thing might occur again. Such a founder of a dynasty was this Sheshonk I, the Shishak of the Bible, who caught up Egypt from her weakened Priest-Pharaohs when they had lost their hold, and proved his strength by gaining control, consolidating the country, and inaugurating a new dynasty with a powerful reign. He was the friend and probable ally of Solomon, and his daughter was one of the wives of that king. Having conquered the always obstinate Canaanite city of Gezer or Gaza, Sheshonk gave it to this daughter that she might appear well in the sight of her husband. We are back of the time of Assyrian greatness. Egypt was still re-asserting her claims in Syria. But Solomon's son Rehoboam did not find favor in Sheshonk's eyes. The Pharaoh harbored his rival Jeroboam for some years before that Hebrew came to be ruler of the Ten Tribes of

Israel, and Sheshonk finally marched against the Judean king, capturing a long list of Palestinian cities. The Hebrew prophets tell the story ruefully, yet with a kind of exultation, not neglecting to point the moral strongly, since it was difficult to keep Israel to the high and abstract conception of her spiritual leaders.

With the life and enterprise of Egypt, temporarily revived by the fresh stream of tribute flowing in from Syria, a building period came again. Sheshonk and his successors constructed this great Karnak court. We recall how his sons and descendants, as Pharoahs of the land and High Priests of the Temple, strove with one another, until the divided house fell.

To the right, past the small temple of Rameses III, which is in the side of the court, we find a door in the wall, close to the second pylon. We pass through it, for on the wall outside is Sheshonk's record of his conquest of the unfortunate Rehoboam, and the list of the cities which he took and gave to Amon. If we cannot read them ourselves, we know that they are there, and we may find them in our Hebrew Scriptures—the Egyptologists tell us that many of the names are the same. There is in particular that town Yenoam, in southern Lebanon. We know Thutmose III, 600 years before the inscription and long previous to the Exodus, had made it one of three captured towns which he gave as an endowment to Amon,—and with which the colossal fortune of the god, which wrecked the state, had begun.

THE HOUSE OF AMON

There is another name on this wall which has an interest for us. Among all the others, Sheshonk took the "Field of Abram." This is the first time in secular history that we find the patriarchal name.

But we leave this wonder on the outer wall, to go back into the court and examine the small and very perfect temple of one earlier than Sheshonk, Rameses III,—set across the side. He was the last great Pharaoh of the real Egypt, the Egypt of the Empire, and appeared a worthy namesake of his great ancestor. But his day, early though it appears, came too late. Disintegration had already set in, in the state. After all, Egypt had reached the limit of her power, she had expressed herself in temple building, the last word had been said. Though the strong arm of Rameses III held back the already weakened Empire, and established the line which his father had founded, there were no new words in which to tell his story. The superlatives had all been used. His records were but lifeless imitations, and these he endeavored to have made as complete as possible. Emulating that other Rameses as a great builder, he raised that splendid mortuary temple, which unmarred by any further Emperors, remains to us as "Medinet Habu" on the western plain. But for some reason, Rameses III did not attempt to add the court to the great hypostyle of his famous ancestor at Karnak. That came two dynasties later. Whether he wished to leave the stupendous majesty of the hall supreme, or to prevent the final crowning of it, who shall say? He built this small, but beautiful temple at right angles to the front of the larger one, as if to forbid the carrying on of that forever. Sheshonk and his successors included this small temple in the wall of their court, like a jewel mounted in a ring.

It is difficult because of the imitations and repetition to know the truth about Rameses III. He stands here as an Osiris before all the pillars of his own small court. Behind are three sanctuaries, one for each of the Theban triad. Rameses III belonged to the priests.

Nevertheless, while Rameses lived, Egypt, the Empire, still appeared to prosper. But a palace conspiracy against his life, brought down his grey hairs in sorrow to the grave.

Is it with a sigh of pity, not only for this sad passing of one of the most magnificent of Egypt's Pharaohs, but for the transitoriness of all things, that we turn away? Yet the temple of Rameses III stands firm and strong in spite of 3,000 years.

We leave the old king in his temple and return to our contemplation of the larger building, where we shall pass, step by step, through the additions of Pharaoh after Pharaoh, reaching front after front of the temple, as it was in ever earlier and earlier days.

This second pylon at the back of the great court was badly ruined, so badly ruined that only the masonry on each side of the door remained in

THE HOUSE OF AMON

shape, propped up by a series of iron brackets which interfered with our perspective view through the temple. The pylon was built by Rameses I more than a hundred years before the time of the third Rameses; and for nearly a thousand years it formed the facade of the great state temple. That we can, at a glance, thus take in a period of a thousand years, thrills us. Poor old Rameses I! He had only time to be great in that which his successors carried out. He reigned only two years. And in the glories of his son and grandson who finished his work, it might easily be forgotten that it was he who planned this greatest hall in the world, using for the back of it, the grand pylon which Amenhotep III had made for the front of the temple some sixty or seventy years before, and setting up his own in front of it. So he planned out the area, though it seems that but one of the columns inside bears his name. This is surely the Hall of Records of the Nineteenth Dynasty; the columns and the walls inside and out are covered with the inscriptions of the three descendants of Rameses I.

The hall in its desolation is not deserted by the Sun-god, but all the more is filled with light. It lies open to the whole day now, the sunshine floods the place. Through the one window which retains its shape intact in the broken clear-story, the light pours as if it found no other inlet. As the sun itself gilds the old, gray stones, we suddenly question, "What's become of all the gold?"

Then we remember Ashurbanipal and the conquerors after him. But there is still color left among the capitals. We look up where they seem like huge flowers in the sky. The sun's rays point out the carvings with startling distinctness; and here and there on the columns we catch, chiseled indelibly deep, the name of Rameses II, that name we know so well. But we shall return to this hall, for the sake of which, now that its other glories are in ruins, the temple is still famous.

It is best at first to gain just the general impression of its greatness, passing through between the columns of the nave and out of Amenhotep's portal into the central court, which was the forecourt of Amenhotep's temple,—where the glorious color is gone; the form alone remains. From here we can go out on the north side where, on the outer north wall of the hypostyle hall is the story of Seti I.

Seti reigned one year with his father, Rameses I, the second and last year of the old king's administration. After Ikhnaton and his successors at the end of the Eighteenth Dynasty had lost the Empire in Asia, and their throne in Egypt, Harmhab, usurper and reorganizer had restored order in the kingdom. Then came Rameses I. It was the dream of Seti, probably inculcated by his father, to recover the Empire. For all that last year of Rameses I's life, Seti was preparing the army. We can imagine it all—how the eager and enthusiastic younger man must have planned it

THE HOUSE OF AMON 111

out with his old father, who knew the actual accomplishment would not be vouchsafed to himself. When Seti came to the throne, all was ready. There had been one year of preparation, there were three of battle:—a campaign against the Libyans on the Western Delta, and two campaigns in Asia, which restored the southern part of the Syrian countries. Then for some reason—perhaps a treaty—he ceased his victorious war, never crossing the threshold again.

The first tribute which he had exacted, were logs of Lebanon, felled under his supervision, for the barge of Amon and the flagstones of the temple at Thebes. There was little wood in Egypt. Seti's cedar souvenirs were safely floated from the Syrian harbors and up the Nile.

Harmhab had before this, begun the restoration of the temples which Ikhnaton had broken. We find Seti still restoring, as well as planning colossal new works, such as Egypt had not yet beheld. It was then that the Empire spoke itself again, and again took shape in the temple forms.

On this wall is the first record of Rameses II, the small person with the minor's lock of hair, close behind his father's chariot when Seti smites the Libyans. It is that little figure which has so appealed to early Egyptologists and lovers of Egyptian history, who once in the wonder of translating, believed all Rameses' stories of his childhood. Now come scholars, with a brighter lamp of learning, and inform us that the cherished little figure is—Rameses indeed, and yet a forgery! It was inserted by Rameses himself—not only upon an original inscription, but upon another little form which had first been inserted over the inscription. The color which covered the changes has disappeared, leaving bare the hard fact. We confess a disappointment. We do not like to lose an illusion concerning our old hero and to accept this story instead. But the light of learning is sometimes hard. And who was the little figure under his, whose form and name are here obliterated? Undoubtedly an elder brother, who had reigned for a day, or perhaps without reigning, had persuaded his father to place him here for his own future reference, but who likewise had not accompanied his father to the war. He is gone—without leaving us his name—nothing but these faint lines, this shadowy wraith. If others were not so positive, we could almost be persuaded that the first small shape which is turned the opposite way, is also a drawing of Rameses himself, which he did not like, and had changed. But here and there in the length and breadth of Egypt, the savants have caught names, perhaps but a portion at a time, which seem to prove that there were not only one, but two princes older than Rameses! Perhaps this first-born died. But if so, and Rameses succeeded naturally, his elaborate statements as to his own appointment as crown prince, which in view of that figure must have been false, would have been unnecessary to establish his claim.

THE HOUSE OF AMON

Those faint lines will insist, not only upon the other boy, but upon some great upheaval.

Ah! many an intrigue was carried through by the aid of the priests of Karnak. Court fictions and priestly tales have often effectually hidden the historic truth from us even today. Of the kings whose usurpation was aided and abetted by priestly intervention, three were among the greatest rulers of Egypt's history: Thutmose III, the Conqueror; Harmhab, the Re-organizer and Lawgiver; Rameses II, the great Builder. Perhaps it was appropriate that his reign should have been brought about and inaugurated by this priestly service.

We return through the ruins of Amenhotep's court, and out at the southern entrance. Around on the south wall of the hypostyle are Rameses II's memoirs. Here is a picture of his famous battle of Kadesh, the first battle in the world whose records enable us to follow the strategic positions of the armies. It is repeated, with the epic song to which it gave rise, on Rameses' pylon to the Luxor temple, and later and best on his Ramesseum, over on the western shore.

A small wall projecting here is an interesting document. On it is carved a copy of the first international treaty, to be preserved for us. It was concluded by Rameses II with the Hittite power, the earliest first-class power with whom Egypt had to deal. With this people, the thrilling Kadesh battle had been fought.

Beyond Rameses' records, is the place, not far from Sheshonk's victories over Rehoboam, where Rameses' son Merneptah, the Pharaoh of the Exodus, cut his own hymn of victory—over *Israel* and others! It has an interesting explanation. As it belongs to a time in Palestine probably before the Exodus from Egypt, Petrie believes that it refers to those relatives of the Hebrews in Egypt, who had remained behind in Syria, and kept up the associations of the old traditions. So the song is important to us, for it contains the first reference to Israel known in history, the Bible records all having been written after that.

While we stood on this side of the Karnak temple, excavating was going on—aided by groups of children carrying baskets on their heads. One group was always here with the baskets to be filled; another was emptying the earth at a distance; another was on the way. They sang as they passed along—a simple procession, when we remembered the priests. There was an unsightly hole at our feet; but it has yielded up many a treasure in the sifting of the earth; small figures which have buried themselves all through the sacred soil and escaped confiscation for two thousand years. They pass now to a museum glory.

Eastward, back of and slightly above our elevation is the sacred lake of the temple, once weirdly surrounded by colossal statues which darkened over and were reflected in it. Away to the south are the several southern pylons, badly broken;

THE HOUSE OF AMON 115

among the palm trees, the gate of the Temple of Mut in the distance. The further two of the ruined pylons were the work of Harmhab, the Restorer, who opened up the way for the Nineteenth Dynasty, the line of Rameses. In his day, the pylon of Amenhotep III, now the back of the hypostyle hall, was the front of the temple, and these new pylons led from the side to an entrance in the forecourt now about midway of the temple length.

It was the priests who declared Harmhab king by an oracle of Amon, on the road between Karnak and Luxor at the great procession of the Feast of Opet, after the state of anarchy and chaos in which the Eighteenth Dynasty had gone out. Gradually the priests of Amon had regained the control of which Ikhnaton had deprived them. Tutenkhaton, one of the weak successors of the idealist, was forced in order to maintain himself, to restore and re-instate the priesthood of Amon, and was in turn compelled by them to change his name to Tutenkhamon.

When several of these weak rulers had followed one another, the general, Harmhab, conspired with the priesthood, who announced him before the people as divinely appointed to reign. Immediately after this declaration, Harmhab went into his palace which was beside the road, and there married a wife of the royal line. This established his claim. As the priestly procession passed before the palace bearing the image of the god, it stopped again to convey the divine sanction and confirmation of Harmhab's sovereignty.

The priests were now ready to wreak their revenge. The pylons of Harmhab are especially interesting to us because they contain the Temple of Aton, which Ikhnaton had caused to be built in the garden between Karnak and Luxor, and in which service once went on when the great temples of Amon were closed. Not one stone of the idealist's temple was left standing upon another. These solid pylons to the House of Amon were made out of the blocks. Today the pylons are almost as thoroughly ruined; and the name of Aton on the stones, turned inward in building, has now fallen outward toward the light.

Harmhab's task, as that of every restorer after every period of disintegration, was the reforming and re-organizing of the state, the construction of a system of government in which the people, even in the smallest and remotest corner, should have their lives arranged and made secure. It was the temple of the state the sovereign reared. The organization, the form to make safe the people's life, is always the gift of those who are high in rank or intelligence. Not Harmhab alone, though he renovated it by a fresh body of laws, but almost all the Pharaohs of the Empire had helped to perfect it. To them belonged, not only the conquest of the Empire, but this internal construction of the state.

Ikhnaton, following the light, had broken through

THE HOUSE OF AMON 117

the conventions of religion and loosed his hold of the laws of the land. Harmhab was not following an ideal, but was looking to his own power and the material welfare of the people. He considered that the conventions of religion and law, a careful controlling organization, were a necessary safeguard, lest the people, lacking themselves in inspiration, and failing to follow the leader who had released them from the bondage of conventions, should fall into hopeless confusion.

It seems necessary to begin every reform through the old forms ere the spirit forms the new. When Israel first went out of Egypt to develop a purer religion, she retained, not only the form of the temple, but the order of the priesthood, with the High Priest as its head. Harmhab, however, was not leading toward any purer religious conception. He was not looking up, but rather down at the organization of which he was the head. In spite of the severity of his penalties, he was a humane man, though—as in our judgments of contemporary statesmen—there are varying opinions among Egyptologists concerning the characters of these old heroes. It was for the sake of the people that Harmhab made his penalties against bribery and corruption extreme. His code was engraved upon a huge stela set up in one of these pylons of the Aton stones.

During the best periods of the Empire, all men for their own dignity, upheld the king, not struggling against one another for position, but chosen by the king for merit.

At the same time with the re-organization of the state, the conventions of religion were again fitted to the people, but they no longer sprang from new life; they were never again more than mere form, though the most elaborate ritual and the largest temple buildings came after. The priesthoods were already revealing their power of influence. Even at this time, there was one organization over the whole land of Egypt, with the High Priest of Amon, of the state temple at Thebes, rising to its head.

Under Harmhab and the earlier Pharaohs of the Empire, the state was managed as a vast estate. The government existed for the sake of an economic prosperity and productivity; and Egypt was handled as crown lands might be today. Yet the Temple, which represented the ideal of the state, was really a counter-organization, already absorbing land from gifts, and, being untaxed in its lands and its wealth, was already disturbing the economic proportions.

Leaving Harmhab and Ikhnaton, we turn back from the southern pylons, and before this southern entrance, we see where a great obelisk once stood. It must have pointed the way toward what is now the kernel of the temple, and toward that line of kings, the mightiest of whom was Thutmose III— toward the secret place, and toward the origin of all the priestly power. Alas, the temple behind it, only too well simulates, in the utter confusion of its wreckage, the great feud of the Thutmosid

THE HOUSE OF AMON

family. They were a house of powerful loves and hates. Yet from them, after Thutmose III, the great warrior, sprang Amenhotep III, the lover of beauty, and Ikhnaton, the idealist.

Thutmose IV, he who uncovered the Sphinx and who was the father of Amenhotep III, found this obelisk of his grandfather, Thutmose III, still lying here unraised beside the entrance to the temple; and acting less as builder than restorer, he caused it to be lifted to the old conqueror's memory and his own. It is not here now, for it belongs to the spoils of the nations. Egypt is scattered through all the kingdoms of the earth. To find this obelisk we must journey to the Lateran in Rome.

When Thutmose IV first raised it, there was not even this court before us, the forecourt of Amenhotep III, with his big pylon and sphinx avenues. This way led across the then front of the temple, the true temple of the Thutmosids, in which they wrote not only such records as they consciously caused to be inscribed upon their memorial walls, but in their very building revealed the stress and strain of their characters. Here the obelisk of Hatshepsut towers insistent over all.

Returning into the court of Amenhotep III, the ancient way across the front of the Thutmosid temple, but now the middle court of Karnak—we find Thutmose I, the father, third king of the Eighteenth Dynasty. We must begin with the first kings of this line and come down, for its later monarchs restored what its earlier Pharaohs built. The pylon, which formed the front of Thutmose I's temple and the back of Amenhotep's later court where we stand, is now a confused and confusing heap of stones. Beyond this, the ordinary tourist can distinguish little in the general wreckage, but the scholars know every wall. Thutmose I began to make the temple sumptuous, though it was with the founder of this Dynasty, Ahmose of Thebes, that the religion of Amon became the state religion, and that what had been a small Middle Kingdom temple, back there where the sanctuaries are, became the temple of the state.

Nearly 2,000 years of history and periods of advanced civilization, lay behind the Empire. Ahmose, having expelled the Hyksos usurpers, and reorganized the state after the fall of the Middle Kingdom, began the restoration of the old temples, using the stone from our familiar quarries near Helouan, which had once supplied the Pyramids.

For the Temple of Amon at Thebes, Ahmose built a cedar barge and furnished an elaborate temple service. But his building energy was scattered throughout the land, and the House of Amon had as yet scarcely perceived its own importance. Amenhotep I, the son of Ahmose, added a beautiful gate to the little temple, but a change in the level of the Nile made it necessary in a later reign to destroy this portal. Then came Thutmose I, and with him began the building of the temple. The small state sanctuary was not

A NILE VILLAGE

worthy the widening importance of the Empire. This Emperor planned to construct a larger building, which should include the ancient chambers.

The width of the temple he made practically what it has been ever since; and all across it—between this broad outer pylon of his and the old sanctuary, he placed his hypostyle hall. The whole was an imposing structure for his day; and he set up his obelisks before the entrance, one of which is that tall shaft now in front of us. The nearest southern pylon, which we have left behind us, at right angles to this front, is also his. The columns which bore the ceiling of Thutmose's hall on either side of the nave, were originally cedar of Lebanon. So that some six hundred years before the building of the temple at Jerusalem, we find the cedar of Lebanon used in the building of the national temple at Thebes, for the columns in the hall before the holy of holies.

In this place originated the power of the priests of Amon; and this ground whereon we stand was the scene of one of the most dramatic episodes in Egyptian history—for within this hall was its builder, Thutmose I, deprived of his throne.

As Breasted gives us the story, in the royal family was a prince Thutmose, who possessed no right to succeed to the sovereignty of Egypt. Therefore was he destined for the priesthood. Such an arrangement, even back in the Eighteenth Dynasty, had the effect, not of giving the royal family control of the priesthood, but of introducing a force from without to tear asunder the family.

In those days there was a royalist party in Egypt, against which the party of the priesthood made its first trial of strength. Of the children of Thutmose I, the only one who grew up with a full title to the throne was his daughter Hatshepsut, the royal daughter of a royal wife. The party who stood for the direct descent overcame all difficulties, and compelled her father to name her as his successor. However, the priestly prince Thutmose was quietly gaining the support of the priesthood. Finally, as was done more than once in the history of Egypt, the coveted position was won by a marriage with the heiress to the title. This was the claim of his own father to the throne of Egypt. In the case of Prince Thutmose and Hatshepsut, it would appear, from a surface view of its effects, to have been purely a *mariage de convenance* of 3,500 years ago.

We cannot tell how this prince and princess may have planned together—or whether, indeed, Hatshepsut desired to wed Thutmose. Considering the insistent qualities, which that youth as a warrior subsequently displayed, we can imagine it quite possible that the old king yielded to strong and subtle influences, and weary of importunities, gave Hatshepsut to the prince. Perhaps also, the king arranged it, to make sure of the descent through his line, since some Egyptians might object to a queen alone. On the other hand, considering also that Hatshepsut herself dominated

THE HOUSE OF AMON

her husband, keeping him absolutely in the background while she lived, and thus proving herself the most royal descendant of her house, we cannot believe that she was married against her own consent.

Neither do we understand whether the father himself was aware of the deepest plots of the prince. But when Hatshepsut's mother died, the claim of Thutmose I, which he had held through his wife, passed by the same law to the prince, Thutmose, whose wife was the daughter of that queen. The moment had arrived. It seems like a fairy tale to us, though to them it was doubtless real enough. The old king in his temple hall, offering to the god upon a feast day before the assembled people; his son with the priests among the cedar columns on the northern side. The procession, as was customary, bore the image of the god from the sanctuary, but it appeared to be seeking among the pillars, until it came to the young prince, who fell upon his face. By the oracle of the god he was led to the spot where his father had stood, and where only the king might be. Thus did the spokesmen of Divine sanction already make and unmake Emperors.

Both the royalist and priestly parties were satisfied. Thutmose III, as he is known to history, forthwith began to reign, while Thutmose I retired to a more or less restful seclusion. At first the new king attempted to rule without considering his royal wife. In the political struggle which immediately ensued, he lost his carefully planned-for power and became no more in reality than the Prince Consort. Hatshepsut, his strong and beautiful queen, was the true sovereign of Egypt. She now began her memorial, that most exquisite, terraced temple on the western shore.

But at this point the reign of the two was broken briefly by that of another brother, Thutmose II, in alliance with the father. Bitterly they turned against Hatshepsut, erasing her name from her own temple and placing theirs upon it. Thutmose I died during the reign of this son; and Thutmose II, perceiving that the real power against him was the party of Hatshepsut, and understanding the situation between herself and her husband, allied himself with Thutmose III. Together they held the government for a short period. On the death of Thutmose II, Thutmose III was again unable to keep the authority in his hands, and was forced to a reconciliation with his royal wife. Again they reigned together, and again Thutmose III disappeared from sight.

Hatshepsut's sun had now risen clear. Her partisans, who would rise or fall with her, took heed to steadfastly uphold her rule. In the reliefs of her new temple, which she now had carried to perfection, it was shown that she had been divinely intended to be Queen, as the child of the Sun-god; her birth, in accordance with court convention and folk tradition, attended by miracles. She is also pictured as nurtured by Hathor, crowned by the

THE HOUSE OF AMON 125

gods, and appointed to rule by Thutmose I. He was recorded as saying, "Who shall speak evil of her majesty shall die."*

The country under Hatshepsut, now entered upon a period of peaceful prosperity, of commerce, of exploration, of building and of art—while Thutmose III did the duties of a priest. Hatshepsut was the first great woman whose name and deeds belong to history. It was at this time that the Priesthood of Egypt had just been organized into a whole, with the High Priest of Amon at its head, and the present High Priest was also vizier of Egypt, and Hatshepsut's devoted partisan—so that the priests also were now with her. It would make an interesting story could we know the real wishes of the old adherents of the family through all these troublous times, and especially the thoughts of the family themselves:—if there were beneath ambitious struggles, contrary personal feelings. We cannot trust the official words of praise or blame. Hatshepsut's favorite was the teacher of Thutmose III's childhood, to whom she gave in trust the education and the fortune of her little girl. Thutmose I's old general had superintended the care of this little one when she was an infant. Also the architect of Thutmose I, who had built the Karnak hall, now constructed Hatshepsut's temple. Whether her father himself, who had carved a path of conquest across Asia to the Euphrates and had established firmly the Egyptian Empire, had been later in the posi-

*Breasted

tion of King Lear, listening to first one and then another of his children, who shall ever say? Though he chiseled out her name in her temple, Hatshepsut erected her Karnak obelisks to him, and made one tomb for him and for herself. But the standard of filial expression in Egypt was high.

That tallest obelisk rising over the wreckage is hers—the top of the other lies here. On that ninety-foot page is inscribed, as a charming American woman expressed it, the first "woman's postscript." For writ large down the shaft is the story of how Hatshepsut raises it to the honor and glory of her father, the great Thutmose I; and at the bottom is the naive addition, "And to my honor and glory too."

The huge blocks had been brought on a barge from Assouan and there were well-nigh a thousand rowers in the boats which drew them to Thebes. The tops were covered with electrum, whose shining, lighted by the rays of the Sun-god, could be seen from afar. One was supposed to flood the North, or Lower Egypt, and the other, the South, with light.

No wonder the traders who now filled the country spread the glories of Hatshepsut over Syria. Well might she have sung:

"The thousand rowers bring my obelisks;
The wandering Bedoui carry my fame."

Strangely enough the Queen set up these shafts in this hall; wrecking it in the process, for the roof

THE HOUSE OF AMON

had to be broken and many of the columns destroyed. Though in her father's name, their shining overthrew her father's hall, the hall in which he himself had been overthrown by Thutmose III; and they cast the place into utter confusion.

The tomb which Hatshepsut made beside her temple on the other side of the river, was not used by Thutmose I. Probably he had made other arrangements—and we know that, not trusting his memorials to posterity, he had, as was usual, provided for his own mortuary service in the temple of Abydos.

When, after a reign of some fifteen years, Hatshepsut died, Thutmose III's resentment toward her was revealed. It was so deep that he not only mutilated the reliefs of her beautiful temple, cutting out for a second time her name wherever it occurred, but he also destroyed or disfigured the tombs and statues of all those who had stood nearest her, including his old tutor and the High Priest of Amon.

The fallen masonry which adds to the débris about us here in Karnak was the sheath he built to hide Hatshepsut's name upon her obelisks. But their clear shining overhead must have constantly annoyed his sight.

When we thought how Hatshepsut's body had not yet been found, we could not but wonder why. Could Thutmose III, Napoleon of Egypt though he became, so violate Egyptian beliefs as to destroy it? That seemed so impossible that we scarcely liked to utter the thought aloud. We preferred to believe that faithful friends, not risking the temptation to this crime far worse than murder, concealed her more securely than even the other royal ones were hid.

Once freed, Thutmose showed himself a consummate general, who carried the advance of Egypt beyond his father's borders, beyond the Euphrates, beyond what was ever accomplished before or since in Asia. Returning from a magnificent campaign for a triumph in Thebes, he was faced with an odd situation. Naturally his triumph took the form of temple festivals, and his glory was made visible by the magnitude of his offerings to the state god. In the hall where he had been summoned to reign and where he celebrated his first Victory Feast, he made the first great endowment to Amon. For it was then that he gave, not only silver and gold and precious stones, but Yenoam and the two other towns of the Lebanon to the state temple—beside much land in Egypt to be worked by his captives. It was not in those days, "He that hath pity on the poor lendeth to the Lord." Giving to Amon was presenting to the temple cities, land, serfs and income. In this way Thutmose III began the establishment of the wealth of this temple and this priesthood far above all others.

But the state had now grown beyond even the new temple of his father, the only fine hall of which was marred and broken by those persistent obelisks of his dead queen. He had himself added to its destruction by walling up the shafts. Doubtless he would have liked to destroy the temple entirely and begin again. But building takes long, and a king's glory is as much in his inheritance as in his own achievement. He magnifies himself in magnifying his ancestors. Thutmose III had his own special temple on the western shore. This temple of Karnak was already the state temple of his fathers, and the place where he himself had been called to the kingship. What could he do with it? It was spoiled for him, yet he could not desert it. He attempted some restoration of the hall, setting up stone pillars in place of the cedar ones, on the northern side where he had stood on that memorable occasion. Then he seems to have given up the hall; and all that portion of the temple. Returning from a second campaign, he turns his back upon all that part which since the beginning has been the front of the building; and plans his great hall of triumph clear across the other end. At the feast of the New Moon, a feast we find also kept in Israel, were held the foundation ceremonies. About the hall and the body of the temple were a large number of other chambers in which Thutmose now wrote his own records, and remembered the kings who preceded him. His list of them is in the National Library in Paris. So, in the temple was also preserved his work as an historian. In addition to this, on the walls has been discovered the first account of a botanical and zoological garden, the garden of the temple where he placed his specimens from Asia. Plants and animals are pictured here, which were hitherto unknown to Egypt. We must not forget that at this time, Luxor was yet an unimportant little Middle Kingdom sanctuary. The avenues of sphinxes and the great garden between the two temples were probably undreamed of. It was for this king's great-grandson to plan those. In his day, Thutmose's festival hall was supreme, and even today it is beautiful, as we discover for ourselves when we have climbed over the hills of difficulty made by the ruined walls of all the inner chambers, and have entered it. The glorious color shines out festive still.

Here ends the first chapter of the building of the temple. We have been through all the divisions, for in passing through the temple itself, we were obliged to begin with the latest. Slowly we wander back and thread the maze around the small Middle Kingdom sanctuary, the kernel of the whole, the centre where all began, which in spite of changes and additions, was the sanctuary until the end. The lily columns of Thutmose III, from the little forecourt of this holy place, are standing yet. The southern one bears the papyrus of the South; the other, the lotus of the North. The priest passed in between them. This division of Egypt persisted from pre-historic days, and the fact that the state temple at Thebes faced west, made it possible symbolically to divide its pairs of obelisks and columns. As we look at the sculptured flowers we realize how, before the beginning, the pre-historic kingdoms had their national flowers, their national colors, their kings, their priests, their temples, and their belief in immortal life.

After Thutmose III, from time to time, the temple was restored and added to. His son, Amenhotep II, put right the hall of Thutmose I, and reported it on the stonework around Hatshepsut's obelisks, and henceforth, despite Thutmose's festal hall, this end was the front of the temple.

We have read the book of the records of the kings, unsealed for us within a hundred years. In the temple we are back in the Empire again. We forget the loss, remembering only the gains. Here we have found the details of a story which lives again. The kings have explained themselves to us. It was not enough that they should build, but in their buildings they should leave their names.

Here, then, was the little structure of Ahmose I, who laid the foundation of the Empire; there, was once the gate of his son Amenhotep I. We return toward the front, in the order of the kings; through the hall of Thutmose I, with the towering memorial of his daughter, the masonry of Thutmose III, and the restorations of the latter's son, Amenhotep II. Outside the southern entrance was the obelisk raised by Thutmose IV. Crossing the court of Amenhotep III, we can look through that southern portal where the pylons of Harmhab contain the temple of Ikhnaton. We enter again the great hall, planned by Rameses I, and partly built on the northern half by Seti.

These are they who preceded Rameses II, and who prepared the Temple. Even Ikhnaton, against what he willed, cut stones for it. And as Karnak, more than anything else, represents what Egypt stood for, so also does Rameses more than any king.

Here in the great hall of columns we rest. Above is that one window in the room, where daylight floods the place. We may wander among the giant pillars, yet the size of the hall defies our comprehension. The largest ever built, it is, because of its time, more wonderful than any ancient or modern building; and, strengthened by the modern world, it will stand when the modern world has passed,—still proudly bearing on its walls the first strategic battle record, the first masterpiece of composition in art, and the first attempt at an epic—and after Rameses' records, on the further wall, with no hint of its significance, the first historic mention of Israel.

From end to end of Egypt, Rameses built, telling over and over his story, and setting up his figure in the most titanic monolithic statues ever produced. It was the result of that re-organization of the state and re-conquest of the Empire which came just before him, and in the beginning of his reign. With Rameses the Empire exhausted itself, as it did in the days of the Pyramid builders. Once it had spent itself on the tombs of its god-like kings; now it gave all it had to the kingly temples of the gods.

Excess of power, like that of Rameses, marks a culmination. The very imitation which follows it, stifles the life that remains.

Egypt had once for all expressed herself in form. Her decadence was necessary, in order that other nations might arise with their contributions to the future of the world. A control for the sake of tribute, only maintained by constant warfare, could not last. In such holding of a state, the peace which follows conquest, must ever be giving way to fresh conquest.

That Egypt as Egypt was to endure forever— that would not have been progress. The history of the world is not a continuous evolution—one thing develops in Egypt, another in Syria. But in the enduring Temple which she built, we shall realize that what Egypt gave us was something apart.

Still in thought, we traverse the ancient avenue of sphinxes to Karnak, Temple of Temples,—at once so ruined and so vast that it defies remembrance, save as an unspeakable greatness. Only in the full moonlight may it be seen in all its splendor, when Hathor's shining conceals the ruin and restores the building by her magic to a more than earthly beauty.

CHAPTER VIII

The Valley of the Shadow

AMON-RE, the Sun, was shining as he shone three thousand years ago. Reflected in the water, the only way that we might gaze upon him, he spread his wings of morning when we crossed the river at Thebes. There were only we two and Aboudi, and the donkey-boys and the donkeys; but the plain was peopled for us. We had come to that shore, the land of the setting Sun, where in the barren cliffs which border the Theban plain, the inhabitants themselves of the vanished city of Thebes, lie deep in the rocks, asleep!

We drew up to pay homage at the feet of the two Colossi who guard the path to the whole of this Western realm, the figures of Amenhotep III. The temple which stood behind them is gone, the yearly waste of waters had subsided, and they gazed serenely on fresh green fields surging to their thrones. We felt overawed again in approaching this king—too mighty to take note of us—he who had thus magnified for the ages, and made lasting, his material form to receive us. He is questioning the centuries, to give his message to that which shall understand. Yet some of the treasures which

THE VALLEY OF THE SHADOW 135

he guards and which have so long been held in Hathor's keeping—Moon-goddess, who is Nature or Love—may not last another hundred years.

As we left the statues we could picture the cavalcade of Bent-Anat, sister of her who found Moses, rise out of the dust before us, coming round from the Valley of the Kings to Seti's University;* and we rode a galloping race remembering how she tried her chariot horses against Paaker's Syrian-bred. So we entered the tortuous way that leads for miles to the heart of the mountains, while the barren heights closed round us, and no blade of grass, no living thing, in all that desert waste, was visible.

Strangest of all strange places is that far-hidden Valley behind the bare mountains back of the Theban plain, mountains which have yielded treasure far more valuable than gold. For here the Pharaohs made themselves fastnesses to be secure to the present day. Their hiding-places have been opened now. The three milleniums during which, inscriptions tell us, these kings believed they were to lie in darkness, have passed over the mountain crests above them; and the graves have yielded up their secrets. Within a hundred years Egypt, with the pictures of her life sealed away quite perfect for us, has been unlocked to the modern world, the buildings opened, the key found to the writing on the walls. The forgotten language is read once more, the ocean of Time is crossed; and the unknown life with all its

*Uarda.

daily customs, its beliefs and its ideals, is seen in paintings, fresh as of yesterday. Herodotus might be deceived by the Egyptians themselves; but through this hidden portrayal of the secrets of their lives, *we know*.

Black holes in the spurs of the hills are the reopened entrances. There were robbers in Egyptian days whose rolling away of the stone from the mouth of the pit was to be feared.

The iron gates of the Committee of Antiquities unclosed before our passes. Electric light illumines the tombs during certain hours of the morning. By what light were accomplished the wonderful paintings and inscriptions, which cover the walls of the passages and the tomb chambers? Doubtless the same strong steady glow by which were done in other parts of Egypt and in earlier times, the work, so perfect in every minute detail, on inner walls of living rock. This, the Egyptians have not explained for us yet.

We entered an opening in the cliff which ends the Valley; and three hundred feet down into the foundation of the mountain our little company penetrated, over a bridge across a once impassable pit to a chamber fresh from the painter's hand. In a deeper place at one end lay the king Amenhotep II, as he had lain since near four thousand years, some centuries before the days of Moses. The lid of the sarcophagus has been removed and we looked upon his face. . . . Suddenly, however, a crowd of tourists surged in upon us with a

OUR ROWERS IN THE LOCK

THE VALLEY OF THE SHADOW

strident-voiced conductor, who shattered the spell and the silence. Yet the king's majesty of repose could not be disturbed—as with Bahram, the great hunter, "the wild ass stamps o'er his head but cannot break his sleep."

We came out into the light of heaven only to go down into another tomb, that of Merneptah, the Pharaoh of the Exodus. His finely carved sarcophagus in an upper chamber has never been used; but upon the lid in the lower vault lies a colossal white figure of the king, in an eternal sleep.

From this barren resting-place we went to that of his grandfather Seti, the most beautiful of the tombs and one discovered long ago, but empty of the king when found.

Through the underground passage of Seti's tomb we descended into the realm of the shades. Upon its walls and chambers before Moses was born, was written with human figures the Egyptian Bible of that time: the story of the passage of the soul after death; and the judgment of God, represented by the Sun, placing at his right hand the blessed, at his left, the damned.

How strange these days of travelling are! Early in the morning we had said: "Today we shall go to the Valley of the Kings," with a vague idea, as is gained from books, of what was in store for us. Afterward, the Valley was an experience, a part of our identity because a memory infused into and transforming our being.

We stood upon a mountain crest with that weird

Valley of the Dead behind us; and there stretched before, the fertile river valley, even to Karnak, "the National Sanctuary," "the Throne of the World," on the other side. The funeral temples of the West lay in a line on the desert's edge below us; and at the foot of the precipice on which we stood was the ravine of Der-el-Bahri with its terraced temple opposite to Karnak, and once connected with it by an avenue of sphinxes, only broken by the silver stream.

Aboudi, standing in his black robes on the edge of the precipice, stretched out his arm, and we listened again to the story of the return of the Pharaoh.

We knew with what care the Pharaohs were laid away, and hidden again from time to time as ancient robbers discovered their hiding-place. Was it not with the intention that those very bodies might again see the light after three thousand years?

But although at the end of this time a key to the Egyptian language had been found, and the records read for a hundred years, the search for the great of Egypt had been in vain.

Those tombs back in the Valley were so many of them empty; and Rameses, the great king, had not been discovered. And then—traces, tokens, began to float down from Thebes to Cairo on the stream of tourists: scraps of papyrus, jewels, sometimes what had been a human hand or foot. Modern Egyptian robbers had made a find and were selling as much as they could, unconscious that

THE VALLEY OF THE SHADOW 139

they were thus forwarding a mute appeal for help against themselves.

Authorities came to Luxor, but nothing could wring from the people the secret which meant for them wealth. At last was found the native family from whom the treasures emanated, but neither bribes nor imprisonment could move them—until one, realizing that they could dispose of no more booty, told for the sake of the reward. And immediately, in the burning July weather, three men, Emile Brugsch and his two assistants, came to Thebes.

They met the surly ruffian. Led by him among the lonely scorching mountains, with a waiting crowd of cut-throats whose secret was to be sold, behind them, Mr. Brugsch and his two assistants clambered around the rocks until, beyond a boulder, was discovered a heap of stones. "That is it," said the robber.

With a hastily constructed tackle the Englishman was lowered unto a pit some fifty feet in depth. What he found in the horizontal passage opening from the pit and in the great tomb chamber at the end, made even this strong man faint. He hurried back lest he lose consciousness in this vast grave and his secret die with him. After what he had beheld he desired to live but one more day at least till his message could be given to the world.

Revived by the air, he recalled the forty royal ones imprisoned in that tomb, and how from their torn wrappings the faces of the mighty had looked upon him. Later, it was seen that so perfect was everything, even a wasp fallen on the flowers on the breast of Thutmose III had been preserved.

And in the corridor lay the second Rameses, Rameses the Great!

That night three hundred Arabs were engaged, squads to work and other squads to watch them; and for four days, night and day, a marvellous procession passed. It bore King Rameses in his royal company, kings and queens and priests, along the crest from which the temples they had reared might still be seen. So they wound down from the heights, to the plain and the boats at the river side. The news of their coming had preceded them down the Nile; and once more, as over three thousand years ago, an exceeding great cry went up from Egypt; all Egypt was in mourning, weeping and wailing for Pharaoh along the river banks.

So the great ones came to Cairo, where they keep perpetual state, saved and brought to the light by alien northerners more than three thousand years after they were interred. Yet,—would they could be shielded from the gaze of the irreverent, even as Seti prayed, in an inscription on his white sarcophagus:

"May the impious not take possession of me!"*

Was it *Death* of which the Egyptians were chiefly conscious—with their figure of a mummy at every feast,—Death which carved the memorials, preserved the very bodies, lasting till today?

*Rawnsley.

The Rosetta Stone has given the clue to the lost language; so that men understand those pictures without background or perspective, yet with meaning in every proportion; know the very sounds of the words; read the inscriptions and maxims. The family relations, even the nurses, poets, architects are known to us; those things which in the great of all ages typify our own relations and make the rulers living to us. More than all, light is thrown upon those Hebrew scriptures, which have become the Bible of our race.

Yet in spite of all our knowledge those closed silent lips of the Pharaohs keep back many a secret, and the more we know, the more we feel the unsolvable mystery of *how* they thought.

CHAPTER IX

The City of the King

IT is still to the temples that we must go to dream of the Pharaohs awake.

Upon another day we visited Der-el-Bahri, the memorial of Hatshepsut, sometimes called Hatasu, royal daughter of Thutmose I.

The name of her temple is thus explained. Many of these buildings were used as convents in the Christian period, and the Arabic word for convent is "Der." Der-el-Bahri, Convent of the North, ancient temple of Hatshepsut, has not been long uncovered.

Terraced to the mountain wall, in the living rock of which its holy of holies is hidden, the temple is a departure in Egyptian architecture and reveals a wonderful sense of proportion, and skill in the outdoor use of the colonnade.

Behind one of these colonnades is the story of the birth of the queen and her nourishing by the goddess Hathor. Behind another is the famous "Expedition to Punt," one of those pictures whose impression is clear and indelible in our minds, not a composite impression, like the "Victories" and "Gods"; because this picture, like the Semitic people in the tomb at Beni-Hassan, like the festival

THE CITY OF THE KING 143

in Luxor, fills in a distinct and separate chapter in Egyptian history. The marvellous skill with which the Egyptian boat is drawn, holds our attention; the cargo, the very fish, the land of Punt with its houses in the tree-tops and its cattle resting beneath—all the story of this voyage of discovery to a treasure country of old is graphically told. The military escort for this temple expedition recalls, despite its different equipment and 3,500 years, the military escort for the Mecca caravan which we saw a month or so ago.

However, the wonderful terraced temple is the evidence that hate as well as love, may be undying through many centuries; for here Thutmose III has left a record of himself in the mutilated places where the queen's figure was portrayed.

Medinet-Habu, that temple of Rameses III, is also to be visited. In its still lovely colors life gleams among the ruins. "Look at the King!" cried Aboudi, before the great symbol of Victory, which we are learning to recognize. "He showing his God all those people he conquered; and he telling his God how much trouble he have in conquering those people." Aboudi, descendant of the ancient Egyptians, has a gentle, melancholy voice which seems to come softly down from a far distance. But it is at the Ramesseum that we hear him best, it is the Place of Rameses that will live the longest in our memories.

All ruined—that Ramesseum. The Committee of Antiquities can place no gates where there are no enclosing walls. Weeds grow among the shattered fragments of the colossal pink statue in the open court. Here and there we find a hand or a foot, which seems as if belonging to some more than human figure. "How are the mighty fallen!" comes involuntarily to our lips—but the power of the mighty remains. The pillars of the temple stand up beautiful in their unprotected desolation. Ruin, the "charm beyond perfection," suggesting always the freeing of spirit, enfolds them in an atmosphere of poetic tragedy.

The first great tower-gate is a fallen heap of stone upon its outside, threatening to let down the whole—yet we trace the carving on the side towards the court. The second gate stands firm and strong, braced by modern masonry; for, more perfect than in Karnak or in Luxor, on its inner wall, close behind the guardian columns of Osiris, facing the inner court, is the greatest picture of Egypt. The first real composition, forerunner of Michael Angelo's Last Judgment, this epic in sculpture and painting illustrates the first epic of literature.

The heroic figure of Rameses, today towers supreme over all his enemies,—not only of that time but of all succeeding ages, and of Time himself. "Ramsie the Great!" said Aboudi. He would not for the world have consciously used a diminutive, for his voice was full of a touching reverence and pride; but the French pronunciation has a caressing, endearing sound, which somehow makes the king human and living for us. In his simple English, Aboudi told of the battle; and we who knew the poem, found fresh pleasure in his telling. He pointed out where the princes and generals were all going the wrong way, leaving Ramsie their king, "alone and no man with him." "He pray to his God," said Aboudi reverently; "maybe his God help him, else how he conquer all those people?" He showed us the conquered warriors fleeing before the single-handed might and vengeance of the king; and a fire and enthusiasm touched him—till we realized that Ramsie was king of his land, and still belongs to him.

Then and there was solved our problem of distracted interest between the Present and the Past. Before that picture in the temple we felt how the Egyptian life goes on much as it did of old; and we found the Past in the Present.

We were no longer even aware of the veneer of Orientalism which has been cast upon Egypt by the Mohammedan religion, for we knew that land as the first country of our Western civilization, its people as the first people of the West. The depths of religion underly us all.

Aboudi revealed to us the realistic humor in the picture; where the hosts fall into the river, and friends on the opposite bank pull them out and hold the Aleppo chieftain upside down to empty the water from his mouth. Those old Egyptians understood that ridicule is the last and deadliest weapon, which leaves nothing of the foe.

There is color in the picture; the river flows blue, surrounding the city of Kadesh with a moat,—one can see the bridge over which the helpers have come to the rescue of the demoralized host. As we looked, the great picture, with its crowd of human figures, absorbed us. We were no longer conscious of ruin, no longer conscious of the weeds in the outer courtyard, of the overthrown statue; we do not know, even to this day, if the picture had suffered any marring, any loss of color; through some magic it was for us as in the days it was accomplished. As we stood and looked upon it so Moses must have looked in the days when the events it protrayed were fresh in the people's mind.

Across the ruined outer court on the outer gate we found the rest of the story: Ramsie again in the battle; all the cities taken; the Egyptian camp and the camp life, where the artist, freed from conventional forms and symbolisms, has given his fancy play among the beasts released from their burdens. And last, by the entrance, sits Ramsie enthroned—the tracing slight yet beautiful. Those princes whom we beheld going the wrong way on the first gate, are approaching to congratulate their king. His face is proud and sad, his hand uplifted as he tells them: "It was indeed the more to my credit, but to your discredit, for you left me all alone!" How human that reproach!

King Rameses!—we have gazed upon his very face in Cairo, not in painting, but "in the flesh,"

THE CITY OF THE KING 147

and this father of Pharaoh's daughter is very real and living to us—even as his pictures and inscriptions all reveal him, from the time when he vowed: "Men shall estimate the strength of the father in me his child;" to this single-handed battle in his own chariot, which fills us with living enthusiasm. Thebes is the city of Rameses.

In the courts of his temple we are enlightened to further secrets of Egyptian art. Those figures of Osiris, in which the king personifies the god, lean against supporting pillars—*they* do not support the roof. Egyptians, though they had developed the column far beyond those early pillars at Beni-Hassan, never used the Caryatides. It is on the same principle that in modern Egyptian mosques the Saracens have not concealed the masonry of arches by ornamental designs, and could not have been guilty of making a wreath of flowers appear to support a heavy weight.

Stirring and beautiful are the whole series of decorations in Rameses' temple. There are other battles in which he is assisted by his sons; and in the library, the room inscribed "the sanctum of the soul," is the tree of knowledge upon which that prenomen, User-maat-Ra-setep-en Ra, is being written. In this room are also the names of sons and daughters, and Bent-Anat receives queenly honors. It all makes clear to us another matter. We remember that in the tombs of the Old Kingdom the guest chambers are decorated entirely with images of the earth-life. At Thebes we think at first that it is ideas alone which live in the tombs of the New Empire. But the tombs in the Valley of the Kings with their dreams of death, are only as the undecorated shaft and mummy-chamber of the tombs at Beni-Hassan and Sakkara. The temples on the western plain before the mountains, —on the other side of which the kings were buried —these temples are the royal guest chambers in which the earth-life is depicted, and the exploits of the kings commemorated in proportionately kingly fashion. That the arrangement is but the old plan magnified is evident from the fact that tombs of the nobility at Thebes are similar to those of ancient Memphis. It was the tombs of the nobility which we entered there—the kings had their Pyramids.

So, in his ruined Ramesseum, Rameses' life, and the forces running through the life of Egypt, are revealed.

Perhaps it is not generally realized that the great picture of Rameses' triumph in his Ramesseum had a hidden romanitc significance. In the result also of the battle of Kadesh, Rameses was the representative of all Egypt, for he sealed the treaty with the Hittite Kheta by marrying the daughter of the Kheta King. Her father brought her to him and she was called in Egypt Ur-maat-neferu-Ra, the whole name signifying "Dawn."*

Womanhood in Egypt from the beginning received higher honor than in other countries of antiquity. Far back in the Ancient Kingdom a

*Petrie.

law was passed which was an advance upon the Salic Law in Europe today; for it admitted women to reign in their own right. Women went about freely as the equals of men. The queen consort was sculptured beside the king. Descent was traced through the mother as well as through the father; and it is the mother who is pictured with her son in his tomb. Family life in Egypt presents many beautiful features. Woman had her place in mythology also. The Sun-myths which personify the Sun and the Moon, or the Sun and the Earth, as a man and a woman, thus expressing the highest rhythm of the Universe, are evident in the Egyptian worship of the Moon-bride of the God-of-the-Sun. Temples were raised to her—Isis or Hathor—Goddess of Nature or Love, with the horns and the Moon for a crown.

This marriage of Rameses, himself the "image of the Sun-god," stands for great things.

A tablet in Abu-Simbel, containing what purports to be a dialogue between Rameses and his favorite god, Ptah, thus rehearses the matter:

Says Ptah:* "The people of Kheta are subjects of thy palace. I have placed it in their hearts to serve thee. . . . All their property is brought to thee. His eldest daughter stands forward at their head, to soften the heart of King Rameses II,—a great inconceivable wonder. She herself knew not the impression which her beauty made on thy heart. . . . Thou art the most complete example of strength and power. He is inconceivably great, who orders and does not obey. Since the times of the traditions of the gods, which are hidden in the house of the rolls of writing, from the times of the sun-god Ra (Re) down to thee, history had nothing to report about the Kheta people, but that they had one heart and one soul with Egypt."

Rameses replies: "Thou has committed to me what thou hast created. I do and I will do again all good for thee, so long as I shall be sole king just as thou hast been. I have cared for the land, in order to create for thee a New Egypt, just as it existed in the old time. I have set up images of the gods according to thy likeness, yea, according to their color and form, which hold possession of Egypt."

Of the daughters of Rameses we know the names of several, including Bent Anat, ("daughter of Anaitis"*) Meri-Amen, and Nebtaui. "A much younger sister named Meri, (Beloved) deserves to be mentioned, since her name reminds us of the princess Merris, the daughter of Maat-neferu Ra, the Kheta princess, who, according to Jewish tradition, found Moses when she went to bathe."†

Strange if it were the little daughter of the Asiatic queen, who found Moses near the university city of On, the present Heliopolis, when the court was in the north, and who in the yearning of her woman's nature persuaded her father to let her keep the baby. Moses was probably educated

---
*Anaitis is the name of a Syrian goddess.
†Brugsch-Bey.

THE CITY OF THE KING 151

at Heliopolis in all the priestly lore of that peculiarly religious city with its Eastern influence, but we may also imagine him brought with the king's sons to Thebes and trained in the University of Seti just beyond us. So possibly it is the school of Moses which we passed on our way to the Valley of the Kings and which we are still privileged to walk through today.

But the half Asiatic daughter of Rameses little knew that she was raising up a great leader of an Asiatic race, who should contend with her brother Merneptah—with whom he may have been educated—and should break forever the bonds of that race in Egypt—nay, who should be the herald both of the Semitic supremacy in the world, which followed the Hamitic and preceded the Aryan; and of the second great development in human thought, the casting away of images and symbols.

No man knows where Moses is buried. But, sitting on the base of a column in Rameses' great hall, we recall the empty tomb of Rameses' son Merneptah, and the close-wrapped body of that king, lying now in Cairo, so still, so eloquent of the passing of the Hamitic power.

With this deeper significance in our minds, we returned to look once more at the picture of the great king, in his lonely triumph. His figure has become to us a symbol of something greater, unlocking for us the meaning of a world of other symbols.

We who have seen the pictures cannot but rejoice this day that Rameses was left all alone; that in his victory, the most dramatic episode in Egyptian history, he might feel himself the incarnation of all Egypt,—nay, in that fundamental virtue; supreme courage, the incarnation of divinity. That picture in the inner court of the temple is full of symbolism, some of which has become conscious and conventional, but in all of which, if we could but read, is the clue to Egyptian thought.

The size of the king, like those heroes, half-God, half-men, in the legends of all nations, is significant, a symbol of his might; still more significant, the evident belief of the king that he was divine.

Symbolism is before language—it is the language of the Beginning and of that which is to be fulfilled. Egypt is the great example, the great country of it. It belongs to childhood and to the first stage of human development, and is nowhere seen as here. Always there is more in it than those who gave it utterance understood.

But—as often since—the images or symbols which clothed God for the common people became so numerous that God, the Truth, was hidden by them—and then did Moses lead the Israelites from Egypt, and give that second commandment to the childhood of the human race, which we learn in our own childhood today. After Rameses, comes Moses; out of the form, the Truth. At Karnak, greatest temple of the world, they are digging up the images against which that commandment was made.

THE CITY OF THE KING 153

Egypt, earnest and religious, with all the symbolism of the Beginning, held a conscious belief in one God in her priesthood. "O thou mighty One, of myriad forms and aspects," says an Egyptian hymn. Abraham also had brought from Chaldea the idea of one God, and his descendants had dwelt in Egypt under Asiatic kings. When later, Moses, the baby of Egypt, the Hebrew found by Rameses' daughter among the reeds of the river, and still revered as a prophet on its banks, was brought up in the highest ranks of the Egyptians and educated in their priestly colleges, he added to his hereditary belief in one God, the knowledge, the expression, and the means of expression, of the priesthood of Egypt. The Hebrews were in a primitive and patriarchal stage compared with their civilized masters.

It was at the height of Egypt's civilization that the Semitic Moses led his people out of Egypt; an event which seemed of no unusual import to the Egyptians. But is was not only a political movement, it was a rebellion against the forms of the old religion, a protest against the symbolic images with which the Egyptians clothed God for the people.

The Semitic Hebrews, white-faced, white-robed, a chaste people, carried their pure white religion, the greatest blessing of the world, through all the vicissitudes of their little kingdoms of Israel and Judah; while Greece and Rome, with their great civilizations, but with mythologies lighter than that of Egypt, rose and declined. And again, just as Rome reached her golden age, the zenith of her glory, a Hebrew, Jesus, brought another reformation, of no moment to the world apparently, scarce a thorn in the side of Rome at first, yet it heralded her end and the birth of Christianity. Christianity, grown out of Judaism, became the religion of fading Rome, and especially of her successor, the young Gothic civilization of Europe.

Today we stand before the secrets of the earliest stage. Today the world reads the other side of the ancient story.

Egypt speaks for the ancient Egyptians. Did the inhabitants have a premonition that the glory of the Hamitic race would fall when it clashed with the full sweep of the later-developed Semitic people? We can understand the hopeless misunderstanding between these alien races. But much that Israel brought from Mizraim has only been learned after three thousand years. The Hebrew writings told us that Moses was educated as a priest. Not until the last hundred years did scholars know that the name, "I am that I am," given him from the burning bush as authority for his message, was the Egyptian name for God.

CHAPTER X

Israel in Egypt

WHAT is the story of Moses from Egyptian records? The relation of Palestine and Mizraim?

Until a century or so ago Christendom has seen the peoples of this age,—these Egyptians, Hittites, Balylonians, Chaldeans, Ninevites—only from within the Hebrew position and point of view. Thus faintly reflected in our partisan minds, they have seemed the monsters of an evil dream.

Now we begin to know them from without the Hebrew consciousness—objectively—nay, more, we begin to find their centres and points of view. For the first time from the ancient world of Western Asia and Eastern Africa; from the dwellers and the travellers over lands and waters, mountains, valley routes and cities, the mists have rolled away. The romances of Thebes, Jerusalem, Nineveh and Babylon are real.

Names have become words with meanings, in which, as we ponder maps of the ancient seats of the mighty, we read the story of the Past, the drama of the world. The peoples live again, the cities take on personalities, as do the gods who represent the geniuses of the nations. In the plans at the back of our Bibles, which illustrate the Hebrew story, we may trace the campaigns of Egypt, reading Egypt under Palestine.

By breaking up and combining the different histories,—Egypt's and Assyria's—with Israel's commentaries and political prophecies, what a vivid living history of those times we have!

To begin with, Egypt was not aware of Israel. The first historic mention of that people occurs in the hymn of victory of Merneptah, Pharaoh of the Exodus, probably shortly before the tribe in Egypt went out. Petrie conjectures that this conquered tribe in Palestine were a branch of the family who had never gone down into Egypt, but remaining had kept up their earliest associations with localities.

Back of the time of their leaving Egypt, the Hebrews in that country were to the Egyptians no more than one of many Semitic tribes, who for trade or as captives had for centuries filled Egypt. The Hebrew story stands clear cut, alone, without historical or geographical perspective, and with no need for such, since it is a psychic drama of human development to which the externals are mere accessories. But in Egypt it is only within the records of larger migrations that we trace the Hebrew story, finding it confirmed and illumined by the movements and conditions revealed.

Of Abraham, the first Hebrew visitor, we have that late and elusory trace in the name, "Field of

EGYPTIAN SUGAR CANE AND HUMBLE EGYPTIAN HOMES

ISRAEL IN EGYPT

Abram," among the places captured by Sheshonk from Rehoboam, and listed on the Karnak wall. Palestinian tradition in those days had evidently marked the spot. In the tomb of Khnumhotep at Beni-Hassan we saw that picture of a band of Semitic people, bringing gifts, which was hailed by its discoverers with enthusiasm, as probably depicting the entry of Joseph's brethren into Egypt. Known now to belong to a period long before Abraham, it portrays the entry of one of those patriarchal Bedouin "Princes of the Desert," as they were called, who drifted westward in a singular and apparently intuitive migration from Semitic Chaldea, and of whom Abraham—since his story tallies perfectly with their description—was probably a late representative.

The Hebrew story is typical.

From the opening of history and before, the Semitic element, as we have seen, was always sifting into Egypt from the East, and through their blood as well as through their ideas, influenced more than we can measure the development of Egyptian thought. We are told that words of the Hebrew dialect are found in Egyptian records 500 years before the Hebrew Scriptures could have been written. The Semitic language, as the language in which intercourse with the other earliest nations had to be carried on, as also, a foreign language whose acquirement implied culture, became at the court of the Pharaohs of the Empire something like French at the courts of Western Europe.

When we come to Joseph, his environment is clearer and explains him better. In reference to the Ishmaelites who sold him into Egypt, it may be recalled that the Arab race today consider themselves the descendants of Ishmael, and assert, though with bitterness, their relation to the Hebrews.

In the long familiar Hebrew records of Egypt, we find the closest harmony with the details, now uncovered, of Egyptian life, at that period when the Hebrews were most closely connected with Egypt. There was that office of vizier, the office of Prime Minister, who held Egypt in his hand for the Pharaoh, who regulated the economic affairs of the country to the smallest detail and the remotest corner, fixing taxes and administering justice. The Hebrews out of Egypt, with time at last to look back, developed to a retrospective consciousness of their own story, saw Joseph in this office. The story conforms perfectly to Egyptian arrangements, for the Prime Minister stood next to the king, and was vested with the real power of the ruler. With a view to the future he was kept informed of conditions as well as of actual revenues. A day in the life of the Egyptian vizier would be an interesting chapter in the story of the state, and would fill in the Hebrew tale.

We are told that each morning he appeared at the palace for an interview with the king. Coming out, he always met the treasurer at the entrance,

ISRAEL IN EGYPT 159

and they exchanged reports. The taxes were not paid in money, but in produce and the granaries formed one of the chief departments of the treasury. After the conference the great man went on to open the court for the day, personally hearing cases and being informed of all business brought to his office. Here he received the reports of all the local administrators.

There is a rank of birth and a rank of office, not necessarily coincident. An official who did well in his little local administration might hear the command to come up higher. At last, in the early days of the Empire, it had come to pass that what counted was not rank of birth but rank of office.

In the story of Joseph's vicissitudes and rise to this position and power, we may see a similar development of Israelitish and Egyptian ideas—and an intimate knowledge of Egypt on the part of Israel. Joseph's adventure in the House of Potiphar was already written in slightly different guise in the Egyptian tale of the "Two Brothers." The story of the Chief Butler and the Chief Baker is illuminated by the Egyptian reports of a palace conspiracy at the end of the reign of Rameses III, after the Exodus, showing that royal butlers who participated in the affair, both as culprits and as judges, were important officers of the king's official household.

Even the story of the seven years' famine and the king's dream, has a strange counterpart in Egypt. On a rock near the First Cataract is a story of a seven years' famine and a Pharaoh's dream, interpreted by his "great wise man," Imhotep, a man whose name was never forgotten in Egypt. It is a late record, but purports to be carrying down the tradition of a period long centuries before Abraham. Seven year famines in Egypt have not been unknown, even in modern history. So, while we do not find in Egyptian records the name of the Hebrew hero, Joseph, these records throw light upon his surroundings, and show the Israelitish picture of conditions to be a true and faithful portraiture.

For ages, but especially during the friendly Asiatic Hyksos dynasties just before the Empire, tribes of Semitic Bedoui, like Joseph's brethren, seeking pasture for their flocks, filtered into the rich Delta country, which the Hebrews, writing of it after the time of Rameses II, called the "Land of Rameses." He had left the strongest and most recent impress upon it for them, and they ignorantly used this appellation, even when their stories went back to a time that knew no Rameses. They also, confirming the distance between the people and the king, seem scarcely conscious of the transition from this "Pharaoh of the Oppression" to the "Pharaoh of the Exodus," since the Egyptian policy was continuous. The very errors of the Hebrew record, like flaws in a precious stone, reveal its genuineness.

Having reached the time of Moses, we have arrived at the culmination of Egyptian glory. In

ISRAEL IN EGYPT   161

the Lebanon valley and about Galilee, near Capernaum and Tabor—the "Dapur" of the Egyptians —over the sites of the later Hebrew occupation, Rameses II fought with the Hittites. After the conclusion of a treaty of peace between the two powers, there was no more fighting through the whole of his long reign. But the labor, as well as much of the wealth of Egypt had been brought in by continuous conquest.

While native Egyptians filled the army, captive aliens did the hard, coarse work. Rameses II, the greatest builder of the Temple was hard put to it, not only for building funds and additional sources of temple revenue, but for the actual labor. It is believed that he impressed the Semitic aliens living in the land, and thus became the Pharaoh of the Oppression. The two treasure cities of Rameses and Pithom, which the Hebrew stories tell of as constructed by them, have within a few years been discovered, built of bricks of Nile mud, some of which bear Rameses' name.

There was nothing yet to differentiate these people to history, nothing to show the mission for which history has since proved them chosen.

From this time on, the history of Egypt, though past its power, has been most interesting to us. There cannot be a story until there are relations. At first it was Egypt alone, then merely conquest of the kingdoms about her; at the last it was international politics.

As to the actuality of the type character, Moses,

we only know from Egyptian evidence that beyond dispute, one at least of the tribes who combined to form the Israelitish nation, had gone down into Egypt and come out from thence, and that they must have had a leader. Also, since they had been in Egypt, the land of writing, and with advanced civilization about them, it is inconceivable that their leader and probably others, had no knowledge of the art of writing. From this time on they appear to have kept their yearly records, as was the custom of the Egyptians—colored in the same way by the personal point of view, but, like those of their former masters, containing a stratum of historical fact. At least, Petrie sees no reason to doubt the gist of these historical documents any more than those of the Egyptians themselves.

In taking up the details of Moses' life, we know from Egypt that the court of Rameses, contrary to that of his predecessors, was in the north, the Delta country, sometimes at that city of Heliopolis or On, where Hebrew tradition places the finding of Moses by Pharaoh's daughter.

The place of Heliopolis was unique, as the seat of the worship of Re, the original god of the Sun-god worship in Egypt, the traditional originator of the Fifth Dynasty, and thereafter father of all the kings, either under his own name or that of Amon-Re. That the king might safely enter the Sanctuary at Heliopolis was, even as late as the time of Piankhi, the proof of divine origin, and

ISRAEL IN EGYPT

therefore right to rule. The priesthood, often in rivalry with the state-priesthood of Amon at Thebes, were an older and more venerated sect, and their university also claimed superiority to all others in Egypt. The scholarship of Heliopolis was different from that of the rest of Egypt. It is more like the Asiatic Semitic culture, and seems, in some respects to prove a predynastic Semitic influence at this place. It was a theological centre, a holy city. Here Hebrew tradition finds Moses, and here also, a Christian tradition brings Mary and Joseph with the infant Jesus. The tree under which the story says they rested,—a sycamore, sacred in Egypt,—is still shown.

The Hebrew statement that "Moses was learned in all the wisdom of the Egyptians" fits in especially well, as we realize now, with their story of his adoption by the royal family; and is borne out by the similarity of Israelitish conceptions, temple forms and priestly orders, to those which Egypt now reveals.

A commentary upon the necessity of Moses' flight from Egypt after killing the Egyptian, is the Egyptian horror of the murder of one of their number, in view of the importance they gave the after-life. Therefore the strictness of their laws concerning this crime.

Of the plagues we know nothing from Egypt, nothing from Merneptah's records. "His tomb was empty because he was drowned in crossing the Red Sea," had said our good Mohammedan guide.

But Merneptah was not drowned. This son of Rameses, named for his favorite god, was a dreamer, a lover of literature, for whom the story of the "Two Brothers" was probably written when he was crown prince. His delicate face, as we know it in sculpture, is almost like a woman's. Rameses' first-born son and those who followed, including Khamuas, him who was High-Priest of Ptah and the pride of his father's heart, died ere Rameses, almost a centenarian, went to his rest. Merneptah's reign, after the long strong reign of his father, was a troubled dream. From the northwest came an invasion, unprecedented from that quarter, which had previously been kept in wholesome fear by occasional advances from Egypt. This invasion is remarkable because of the identity of the allies who joined it, who were undoubtedly southern Europeans.

These, therefore, step into history in the same reign as the Israelites. From which direction they came appears to open up the whole question of the origin of our Aryan race. Were they part of a great southward movement, which included the prehistoric Libyans themselves? This would agree with the theory of our Baltic origin, and with the southward changes of historic times, which certainly mixed Aryan blood with the Libyan stock. Or, did they come from Northern Africa, west of Egypt, and later migrate northward to Europe? This would give us the African origin. Either explanation followed to its extreme makes

ISRAEL IN EGYPT 165

us more closely related with the Libyan Kabyles who are brothers to the Egyptians, past and present,—than has generally been supposed; since these have long been classified as Hamitic peoples. Though we have elsewhere spoken of the Egyptians as "Oriental" it was only in their present religion and mode of life. According to the earliest theories, all the white migrations came from Asia; and as for the religious instinct, we find it fundamental in all humanity. The great distinction between East and West has always lain in the psychic interests and development of the one; and the scientific and material development of the other. To the West, the form has always been the first necessity,—there must be a body, even for the resurrection. Egypt conforms perfectly to this Western distinction. And not only is the development of Western civilization continuous from Egypt to present Europe and America, in science and material symbols; but the race which, in Egypt, reached and passed its culminating culture, before the development of any other people, appears to be that same Iberian or Berber race, which has left its monuments and obelisks in Europe, and which,—whatever its migrations, underlies all Europe and Northern Africa. Because it thus seems to be the foundation of Europe in every way, we can hardly speak of it as "Oriental," but we may call it "Hamitic"—though the strong lines drawn by earlier scholars upon the Hebrew Genesis, seem to grow faint as research progresses. The savants are not yet agreed among themselves, and we must wait.*

In Merneptahs time the Delta was overrun and devastated. Merneptah's defence must have been strong, for he was splendidly victorious. But he was an old man, and this makes it easy to understand his dealings with Moses—on the one hand his fear, on the other, his eagerness to hold the valuable bondsmen.

The route of the Israelites out of the country, and the parting of the waters is now understandable. There was a line of forts running north and south across the eastern approach to the Delta. In the reports of frontier officials we read of a Semitic tribe passed into the country only a few years prior to the Exodus; and in the reign which probably followed the event, is the record of the pursuit of some fugitive slaves over the frontier. The Israelites were afraid of being stopped at the forts and accordingly turned far south.

In those days were lakes, north of the Red Sea, which at flood tide and under certain winds, were connected with it. Was the tide more than ordinarily low and the wind favorable, when the

*Everywhere in Europe and among the Kabyles, the Berber is mixed with the Aryan stock today. But the pure stock of the first white race, which in Europe is supposed to have followed the yellow —from which it might seem to have retained its ancestor-worship— is brown-complexioned or even dark in color. A dark skin does not necessarily make a black man, as we admit in the relation between the Hindoo and the European Aryan. Structural affinities permit more scientific classifications. Nevertheless, these historic discoveries reveal to us not only the continuity, but the unity of human life.

ISRAEL IN EGYPT 167

Israelites, light of burdens, light of heart in their belief, passed over "between two walls of water?" And when Pharaoh's heavy chariots tried to follow and sank in the loose sand, the flood tide which caught them, following an ebb so low, would naturally have been unusually high. Some troops may have been lost. The Egyptians do not record their failures.

In the desert beyond the Mokattam hills, is a split in the stone stratum, which forms an ancient well, now popularly associated with this story as the place where Moses' rod brought water from the rock. At least the story is typical of the great need. of Egypt and the East through all the ages, the need for water, which these long-time inhabitants of the Delta, now faced for the first time. Was there anything unusual about the finding of the water? Who can deny? To be able to find a place where men might dig a well for a caravan route, was one of the most fundamental gifts in ancient Egyptain days, and seems to have pertained especially to royalty. It is today asserted in the East that a sixth sense exists in some persons, whereby through the feeling of a twig in the hand, they can divine where water may be found— and Moses must have been in a condition of intense exaltation. Science, by which we have denied as fairy tales the simple stories of childlike peoples, may in time lead us to understand and be ashamed. We have not reached the end.

The difficulties the Hebrew leader found are

now shown to be only too evidently the natural outcome of the age and situation. In the Delta country Ptah had been worshipped in the form of a bull. The masses of the people could not be held to the height of their leader's conception of God, and the mission he evidently foresaw for them. They, like the masses always and everywhere, sought for a tangible and definite form; and when Moses left them to commune with the Most High, they hurriedly made for themselves a calf of gold! There were many times of discontent, of lack of faith, of longing for the security of their work, of which they promptly forgot the pain.

In the plan of the tabernacle and the later temple, we see clearly a form belonging to Egypt—and also to Assyria—perhaps in all these cases the result of a combination of the outer influences of these nations upon one another, and the inner intuitive development of all.

The first ten laws of the Hebrew people, the basis of all that followed, were engraved on tables of stone which would correspond to the Egyptian stelæ—such as that of the great lawgiver, Harmhab, of some hundred and fifty years before. We see how the first two commandments, embodying the idea of the exclusiveness of God, and doing away with images, were necessary for the development and preservation of the great idea of Spirit, which was the Hebrew's mission; and for which their own leading out of Egypt, and their seclusion were also a necessity, if they were to give light to the world.

After that long wandering in the desert, in which they were purified, gradually losing the most limiting influences of Egypt, the new generation came to their own and to national union. In the effort to establish themselves we find them in collision with those peoples whom we have learned to know: the old and mysterious power of the Hittites, already waning; the buffer state of the Amorites, between Palestine and Syria, long the boundary between the Hittite and Egyptian powers; and lastly, the new Philistines. The Philistines appear to be late comers in Asia, also moving south. Their own pottery and the Egyptian description of them as a "people of the sea," harmonize with the Hebrew tradition that they came from Crete,—the true meaning of the Hebrew name "Caphtor." Were they, as has been suggested, Europeans, part of a southward movement, overlapping and submerging the preceding wave of the Hittites?

Just previous to the entrance of Israel into Palestine, the Philistines appear to have pushed south, smiting and breaking up the Hittite confederation, whose strength had already departed, and crowding a fragment of these, with the Amorites, whom they also defeated and displaced, down into Palestine, where they all together barred the Hebrews' way. But the Hebrews were a young generation, and nationally also in the youthful period of conquest which precedes secure establishment. Gradually they made their way into the country and settled there. But straight across the already historic plain of Megiddo, from the Jordan to the sea, the Philistines built a line of cities cutting the Hebrew tribes in two. It almost prevented the Hebrews from acquiring the strength of union and a national existence, and nearly made a Philistinian conquest of them.

However, we know that the Philistines did not crush the Hebrews. The latter achieved their union and their kingship under Saul and David, and smote their powerful neighbors. In Israel, as in Egypt in the glorious days of Empire, the citizens were soldiers; the stranger within the gate was called upon to work. Then, as always after conquest, came the period of prosperity and glory, and the building of the Temple. The "House of Yahveh" or Jehovah, the Israelites called it, as the Egyptians called it the "House of Amon," or "Ptah." "The Palace is not for man, but for the Lord God," says David the King. And we remember how the Egyptians built of stone their temples to the Everlasting, while their own ephemeral palaces were often of brick and wood.

The temple was the visible form to contain their ideal, the sign to suggest it. But the Hebrew conception had come out from the others and was high.

Solomon, from the fulness of his heart, exclaims, "Great is our God above all Gods! Who is able to build him an house, seeing the heaven, and the heaven of heavens, cannot contain him? Who am I then, that I should build him an house, save only to burn sacrifice before him?"

However, to the intuitional mind of Samuel, Jehovah had said of David:

"He shall build me an house, and I will establish his throne," and the heart of David in the silence, had responded. The establishment of the national government and of the national ideal were almost coincident.

In the same way, we find each king in Egypt building on the "National Sanctuary."

But David, as a man of conquest, was not permitted to actually build the Temple of Jehovah in Jerusalem, though he might plan for it. During his reign, he appointed with impressive ceremonies, the crown prince, Solomon, as the crown princes were appointed in Egypt; but this inauguration announced a special mission, the building of the Temple. David the King, said to the people:

"He (Jehovah) hath chosen Solomon, my son, to sit upon the throne of the kingdom of the Lord over Israel."

Israel's kingdom, too, was the domain of Israel's God; but Israel's God alone, did not fall with Israel.

To David and Samuel, so simple, so childlike, might well have come Divine intuitions. The king feels that the Lord gave him the plan of the Temple—whether as a forgotten recollection out of Egypt, or by a similar subjective development, can we say? David, like the Pharaohs, headed the gifts to his God. Gold and silver, brass and iron and precious stones—the wealth dedicated to the Temple was his offering to the Lord. Not yet had come the realization to the human consciousness; "He that giveth to the poor, lendeth to the Lord." Nevertheless, as Jesus showed in reference to the box of precious ointment, our own development demands that we look up and do homage to that which is greater than ourselves.

The satisfaction of building churches, even today, supplies a need which cannot be ignored, which opens our hearts to something higher than food and drink and even man. It has been the keynote of history, this need of the spirit to express the emotion of reverence, to turn to a known or "unknown God," a Creative Spirit which upholds it. So may we sometime realize that exalted conception of humanity, "Ye are the Temple."

When the acts of David were finished, and written, "with all his reign and his might, and the times that went over him, and over Israel, and over all the kingdoms of the countries," Soloman sat upon the throne of his father.

And now we find a great spirit of brotherliness between Solomon of Jerusalem, and Hiram of Tyre; and Hiram sends for the Temple of Solomon's God, skilled workmen, and the cedar of Lebanon, which for so many centuries had gone as a gift to the Temple of Amon at Thebes.

The national Temple at Jerusalem was built

with the great outer court, beyond which was the "holy place for the people," corresponding to the hypostyle hall, and behind this, the "holy of holies." The walls were overlaid with silver and gold. There were two pillars before the building, in place of the two obelisks of Egypt. There was no holy lake, but there was the font in the court. The symbol of purification is a world symbol. There was the altar for sacrifice in the outer court, and there were gold and silver vessels for the service of incense. On a table in the holy place, was the shew bread, left in the Temple, much as Egyptian offerings were left, but with more consciousness of a symbolic significance. Today we have the Table of the Lord, in that most spiritual conception of the Last Supper in the Christian Church.

But the one all important difference between Egypt's temples and Jerusalem's, was the fact that here in the sanctuary was no image of God. The Hebrews realized that God, as Spirit, is not a material form.

In the midst of all the forms about them, we realize as never before, how great was Israel's formless Idea. The highest conception of truth in Egypt had been Ikhnaton's literal representation of the objective world, which after all, is but relative truth; Israel saw inner righteousness, progress toward Spirit. How amazing the smallness of Israel, the greatness of her mission! "Thy people, whom thou hast redeemed *out of Egypt.*"

Little Palestine—redeemed out of, but protected by Egypt! Thus only, could she rise secure among the powers warring for conquest around her.

For in the days of Israel's national flowering, when the national character and the national ideal became established in the state and in the temple, Sheshonk, reviving Egypt, which no longer controlled the Syrian countries, was Solomon's friend and apparently his suzerain in a protective alliance. Sheshonk's daughter became Solomon's wife, whom, as the Hebrews quaintly remark, Solomon felt it necessary to remove from the Holy City of Jerusalem when the Temple was built, and whom he accordingly lodged in a fair palace at a distance.

Alas, Israel, having perfected her Idea, quickly passed into a period of decadence. She lost her pure conception—following after the strange gods of the races mingling with her own. "Because thou hast harkened unto these"—threatened the despairing prophets. From this time was the nation divided—and Sheshonk sided against Solomon's son. Egypt still compelled for a time the allegiance of Palestine, asserting her authority and securing the tribute by occasionally making kings —seating a younger brother in an elder's place. But the greatness of Egypt was now itself forever past—and had become among the nations a dangerous memory. It was but the deluding semblance of itself, the trust in which meant sure disaster.

ISRAEL IN EGYPT 175

Assyria and Babylon were to gather the flower of Israel—but not at once. As Assyria's power grew large in the East, and she gradually included those marginal nations, the possession of which meant Empire, the Hebrew kingdoms, with the others, submitted. But again and again, in her own struggle to escape destruction, Egypt, through envoys, stirred the Syrian states to revolt.

Israel and Judah, through all their existence, had always a hankering for the fleshpots of Egypt. Remembrance of Egypt's greatness was bred into them as into no other of the nations—the others had merely felt Egypt's chastisements. The Hebrews, after their own emulation of greatness, forgetting their former hardships, due to Egypt's power, and eager for friendship with the nation to which they had once appeared contemptible, looked back with longing admiration. Israel, listening to the voice of Pharaoh, revolted with the other Syrian kingdoms and met deadly punishment. For the Pharaoh's auxiliaries sent in aid of the alliance were swept away by the Assyrians, and the Ten Tribes carried into a captivity from which they never returned. (722 B. C.) After that, Judah held steady for a time. The new Ethiopian Pharaoh again attempted to stir up trouble, the Egyptian party in Judah waxed strong. It was then that the prophet Isaiah uttered his immortal protests and held Hezekiah faithful to Assyria.

"Woe to the rebellious children," cried Isaiah in

the time of Hezekiah, "that walk to go down into Egypt . . . to strengthen themselves in the strength of the Pharaoh, and to trust in the shadow of Egypt!

"Therefore shall the strength of Pharaoh be your shame, and the trust in the shadow of Egypt your confusion."*

Shortly after, Babylon arose within the Assyrian domain, and again made trouble among the small states. Judah and Egypt joined the alliance against Assyria. This was the occasion of that vengeful visit of Sennacherib, when Phoenicia and Syria fell, when under Taharka the full Egyptian army, meeting for the first time the Assyrian, was completely defeated, and Jerusalem was scornfully invested,—the ambassadors of Sennacherib uttering those taunts concerning dependence on Egypt, that "reed, upon which, if a man lean, it will pierce his hand." But Hezekiah was not leaning on the reed, he had long turned his heart to the God of the prophet; and when Sennacherib, having conquered Egypt, brought up his army and renewed his taunts by letter, Hezekiah spread the letter in the Temple. Sennacherib's great army was smitten by malarial winds from the Delta, to which they were unaccustomed. And this dire disaster, together with news from Babylon, caused Sennacherib unceremoniously to depart. The deliverance of this one little city *was* remarkable, even from an outside point of view.

*Isaiah XXX, 1: 3.

ISRAEL IN EGYPT

Such were the world politics of 700 B. C., roughly divided between the nations who took sides with the one or the other of the two first class powers, the one already broken, the other, just coming to its strength. Babylon, in alliance with what became the later kingdom of the Medes and Persians, was just rising.

By three generations, Judah, in spite of the despairing efforts of the prophets, had fallen completely from her pure conception and had lost all her strength.

In Egypt the last Restoration had begun with the last strong dynasty. Pharaoh Necho re-asserted Egyptian authority over the Syro-Palestinian nations, and for a time all went well. Then appeared Nebuchadnezzer, King of Babylon, and wrested away the Empire. Presently Judah rebelled against him. "But the King of Egypt came not again out of his land; for the King of Babylon had taken from the river of Egypt unto the river Euphrates all that pertained to the King of Egypt."* Nebuchadnezzar besieged Jerusalem, carried away a portion of the people with the king, and placed the king's uncle, whom he called Zedekiah, on the throne. But Zedekiah, nothing heeding of the lesson, nor of the sovereign under whom he held his throne, also "rebelled against the King of Babylon." Then came Nebuchadnezzar the third time. In vain did the prophet Jeremiah protest and plead that the king and the

*2 King, 24: 7.

princes would go out to the Babylonian ruler, and all would be well. For a time the king shut him up in prison to keep him from weakening their army. Finally, unable to stifle his voice, the princes threw him, as a bird of ill omen, into a mud dungeon in the prison. The king, with fear in his heart, secretly rescued him, secretly listened again to his prophecies; but, unable to oppose the leaders of his people, pursued their policy, to the utter destruction of Jerusalem and of the temple which had stood 400 years. The gold and silver and brass were carried away for the Temple in Babylon. Of the people, a small remnant, chiefly of the poor, were left to till the ground and dress the vines; and a governor was placed over them. Jeremiah also was left behind, and poured out his "Lamentations" over the ruined city. Then again, that Egyptian party, failing to realize that it was their own political error, which was at least the secondary cause of their disasters at the hands of the Eastern Empires, insisted upon leaving Jerusalem altogether, and going down into Egypt to find safety in that country. They carried with them Jeremiah, still violently protesting, and he perished there.

Today, in surveying the whole story, we have understood the violence of despair of Isaiah and Jeremiah at the strength of the Egyptian party whose rebellion wrecked Israel; we have measured to some extent the danger against which Hezekiah prayed when he spread Sennacherib's letter before the Lord in the Temple.

ISRAEL IN EGYPT

With the story connected and illuminated, we can feel a human interest in the action or the waiting suspense of these human beings through each incident. And following the international politics of those days, we understand Israel in the light of Egypt's records, Israel's God in the light of Egypt's gods.

We can see so well how it was in those days of intense subjective feeling, and of distorted outer knowledge—how necessary for the prophets to, use such language to hold Israel from Egypt; how, in order to preserve and to develop their majestic conception of God, the God of Israel, it was necessary that they should not recognize that God in any images or forms.

What partisans we who read only the Bible, have been—and with reason! For those who today read the words of the inspiration of the prophets only from within the prophet's point of view, perhaps come nearest, after all, to the true feeling, and therefore to the true appreciation of them.

One of Prof. Petrie's recent discoveries in Egypt was a very perfect Jewish temple, perhaps of the time of Jeremiah. On the Island of Elephantine there was found about four years ago, by the Berlin Papyrus Commission and edited by Prof. Sachau, a great quantity of papyri in Aramaic, the dialect in which Nehemiah, Ezra and Daniel were written, the popular tongue which Jesus spoke, Hebrew being only employed as a ritual language by learned men. These Jewish documents belong to the Persian era, but as two of the Jewish military divisions which they describe bore Babylonian standards, that fact, together with other strong evidence, proves that here was an earlier Jewish colony, added to by those who came down into Egypt at the time of the destruction of Jerusalem. Though they retained the name of Jehovah (Yahveh) as their national God, they did not see him as universal, and mingled his name with that of other deities. But their temple was to Jehovah.

We recall how Isaiah's prophecy of Egypt's decadence had been fulfilled in detail: "I will set the Egyptians against the Egyptians: and they shall fight everyone against his brother, and everyone against his neighbor; city against city, and kingdom against kingdom." We know now how truly this had come to pass.

And Isaiah had said also: "In that day shall there be an altar to the Lord in the midst of the land of Egypt, and a pillar at the border thereof to the Lord."

(Here at the Island of Elephantine was the "border" of Egypt for many centuries.)

"And it shall be for a sign and for a witness unto the Lord of hosts in the land of Egypt," had continued Isaiah—"he shall send them a saviour and a great one, and he shall deliver them.

"And the Lord shall be known to Egypt, and the Egyptians shall know the Lord in that day."

When the Babylonian Empire succumbed to

DOWN BY THE RIVER

ISRAEL IN EGYPT

the Persian, the Jews were released from the Babylonian captivity. It is interesting to notice the Hebrew story of Daniel's interpreting the king's dream in Babylon, as Joseph, perhaps a millenium earlier, had done in Egypt. Hebrews would seem several times to have been trained at court, at the two great centres of the ancient world.

The new Persian Power was very favorable to the Jews. Cyrus sent back a portion of those who had endured the Babylonian captivity, to Jerusalem to rebuild the city and the Temple. There in chastened spirit they renewed their ideal; there they made ready to give their supreme message to the world. The Persian Empire was wisely welded. Egypt herself became no more than a portion of it, conquered by Cambyses.

As the Persians had encouraged the rebuilding of the Temple in Jerusalem, so they spared the Jewish temple in Egypt, and allowed the Egyptian Jews to keep their Passover in the month of Nisan—the first month of the civil year, as adopted from Babylon.

This, then, is the story of the Old Testament relations of Israel to Egypt.

We know that the subjective revelation which has come down to us dawned first in the East, in Asia, from whence came Abraham, the land which the Egyptians, perhaps unconscious of the reason why, called the "God-land." But Egypt had her own early vision and drew upon the East, giving her ideas form.

And Israel for the pure idea of Spirit broke through the form.

Our broader stories, while they explain Israel, make her more wonderful and living. Lebanon has a new meaning for us, and the deeper meaning of little Palestine in the Jordan Valley is revealed.

It was a chosen country for the religion of the future to come out of, the key to the world, with Egypt on one side and Assyria-Babylon on the other; drawing upon both at first, and then the battle-ground of both; fed by the two great rivers of civilization, the Nile and the Tigro-Euphrates, until it became the meeting-place of the waters, and was submerged.

But its message was carried. In our objective, self-conscious, scientific knowledge of today we can see how the Spirit, subjectively known, was being revealed through it all. The East prepared the message for the West, even as the West prepared the form for the East.

As Isaiah triumphantly concluded:

"In that day shall Israel be the third with Egypt and with Assyria, even a blessing in the midst of the land:

"Whom the Lord of hosts shall bless, saying, Blessed be Egypt my people, and Assyria the work of my hands, and Israel, mine inheritance."

CHAPTER XI

The Evening and the Morning

AN English scholar, versed in sacred nomenclature, has stated that the very name of Israel is made up of three principles: Re, the masculine and material, signifying Egypt, as personified in Egypt's chief god; Is, the feminine psychic element, standing for the goddess, who was the chief deity of Assyria; and El, the general principle.

To the Greeks, whose poetry was so sublime that it took form in gods and goddrsses, the Soul was feminine, was Psyche.

The West, from Egypt to the present day, has developed material science, has been conscious of the form, as expressed in that olf Egyptian hymn, "O Form, One." But the East has given religion to the world. And even as the masculine is attracted by the feminine, the West has always felt the fascination of the East, since the time of Abraham, when the Egyptians saw that Sara was "very fair."

We have observed how, in the mythology of Egypt, the Moonbride of the God of the Sun, expressed with him the supreme rhythm of the Universe, in the figures of a man and a woman. She was Isis, or Hathor or Unit-Goddess of Nature or Love.

Rameses II, Son of Re, and image of the Sun-god, representative of all Egypt, married a princess who, as the seal of her father's treaty, stood for her people; and this marriage symbolized the union of the first two great nations. She was the princess whom the Egyptians called "Dawn."

We are inclined to think that because of its very masculinity, the West has ever since enthroned womanhood.

It was the daughter of this princess who is traditionally supposed to have found Moses, the spirit which broke through the form of Egypt, and heralded the fall of the Hamitic and the rise of the Semitic power.

But to understand all that the form has meant, we must look to the end as well as to the beginning of the Egyptian story.

Just before the Persian era there had come to Egypt, as we have mentioned, a curious Restoration. The Assyrians had not been able to hold the land. They were struggling against Babylonia, rising again to supremacy within their own borders, and against the new Persia or Elam, still further East. Then Egypt quietly dropped away and was gathered into the hand of Psamtik, the Libyan, Prince of Sais. He had dreamed of a reunited Egypt, and the dream belonged to his line. Internal change had always been working

EVENING AND THE MORNING 185

and Libyan generals of Libyan troops, hired in the time of Rameses III, when the temple was absorbing the state, had risen to strength and importance. The city of Sais, often re-inforced, appears to have been the centre of Libyan influence and possibly the seat of a Libyan king, in pre-dynastic days.

By the aid of Greek mercenaries who frequented the Delta ports, Psamtik overcame the prejudices of his rivals; and before all his purpose was fully evident to the world outside, Egypt revived again in the strength of union.

Egypt revived, but her strength was no longer from within. She was held together and maintained against the world by aliens. The state was a more or less artificial organization; for a large body of the army were Greeks, naturally much favored by the Pharaoh, since they brought him his throne and maintained it for him. To a certain extent, the state will be what its army is.

This Restoration was not a new dawn, but an after-glow; the sunset went back to the dawn which had been. With the element of force drawn from without, the purely Egyptian influence was altogether priestly. While Psamtik and the power of the state reach out toward the modern world which is now above the northern horizon, entering into friendly contests of inter-communication in commerce, with its international policies and protections, the Egyptian retires to the remotest beginning, when Egypt knew no world outside of the

Nile Valley. Still Egypt was made by and divided between the army and the religious orders.

The Egyptian went his own way—in the temples. From his limited position, he could not see the economic and political use of the Greeks, who had become necessary to the state and indirectly to his welfare. For the government of Egypt had never grown from out the people; they were lost in miserable chaos and mutual destruction, as the undeveloped classes of all ages must be, unless held by a strong ruler, or a government of able representatives ruling in accord with law, when they live and work in peace. The necessary fighting was now done for the native inhabitants by these foreigners. Yet, so far as Egypt's individual existence was concerned, the priests and the Egyptian party of those days were right. They had lost hold of their birthright. When the power which held Egypt together was alien, Egypt not only ceased to be Egypt for the Egyptians—it ceased to be a true and independent state. That Egypt had perished long ago—with Amon—in the feudal conditions of vassalage, which preceded the Restoration.

Yet the Restoration accomplished, unconsciously to itself, as all greatest things are done, an invaluable purpose. The real Egypt had worked out the beginnings of objective knowledge and self-consciousness, and had wrought them into stone. But this earliest of all nations was the most conservative. The Egypt of the Restoration was the mediator between the old and the new; the interpreter of Egypt to the world, as Breasted's History makes clear to us. In this way the ancient conservative Egypt became the teacher of the infant states of Europe.

Before the day of Psamtik, Egypt had been like Europe in the Middle Ages, a system of vassalage. And now, with more stable government, the scholastic period set in. After all, though the force was imported from without, it was still the priests who gave the form to the state. They alone, in their temple fastnesses, had conserved an ideal which had blossomed into the Restoration. It was not a vision of the Empire. That was too near,—they thought they knew the faults which wrought its downfall. But they dreamed that the state, as it emerged in the beginning, had been perfect. If the forms could be brought back, the same inner-world which once gave life to them would exist again. (How should they know that the classic age is always that preceding the settling of the state!)

But the first great difficulty lay in the fact that the language of Egypt, during three thousand years, had naturally developed. Old Egyptian must have been more difficult to the man of Psamtik's time than Old English is to us. Much of the symbolic character of the early picture-writing had become obscured. It was this obscurity which increased the fascination of Egypt's mystery to the Greeks. Yet the old hieroglyphics contained all that the Egyptians must know to reform Egypt.

Accordingly the ancient language became sacred, and the first instruction the youth received in the schools, which of course belonged to the priesthoods, was to read and write the ancient script. Culture became the study of what had been long left lifeless. The old religious texts were copied for us. Some the scribes did not then understand, but the scholars of today who read the copies, know and correct the mis-reading of twenty-five hundred years nearer the date of the originals.

Though the officials, who proudly bore all the most ancient titles of Egypt, often could not understand the ancient language, yet whatever the affair of the present, the deciding word came by way of the priests from a past at least two milleniums old.*

More conventional than conventions established in the beginning were the forms and the organization of the Egypt of Psamtik's day, because they did not spring directly from new life. In the religious phase of the Restoration we find formalism carried to that excess which tends to its own destruction. Animal worship now became fanatical. And the exact observance of the form of ceremonial purity goes back to the standard of the Old Kingdom before the ethics connected with the Osiris myth had developed. It is the same sort of ceremonial observance which Jesus later

*Breasted.

found in the Hebrew Restoration and which he so strongly condemned.

But the presence of life in Egypt was still revealed. The Egyptians were always artists, for was it not they who first expressed their thought in form? Out of the very ordered condition of things, Egyptian art alone now sprang with new freedom to one supreme last flowering.

Altogether, with its impressive organization, its old customs and its new art, this was a most favorable period for the Greek to grow in Egypt. The time approached the classic age in Europe. And Greece had decayed before Egypt passed away—nay, Egypt, the beginning, has not yet passed away.

Apries, Pharaoh of Psamtik's line, the "Hophra" of the Hebrew records, whose great palace at Memphis Petrie has just been unearthed, stirred up revolt among that unfortunate little group of states, which was usually the margin of one Empire or the other.

But his own native Egyptian soldiers rebelled against him, because of his dependence on the Greeks. And when his general, Ahmose, the "Amasis" of the Greeks, the last usurper and law-giver,—for the two go together in Egypt,—gained the throne by the aid of the native troops, he restricted the Greeks to Naucratis, where, though no longer permitted quarters in other cities, they now had their own. Naucratis became the place of the unity of Greece—such unity as the Greeks never knew in their own country. Here men from Athens, Sparta and the Islands beyond the Seas, erected a common temple.*

The Greeks now take up the story of Egypt, and from this point on, as if the Providence working through the human race had planned it so, the monuments of this period, less needed than those of a former time, have perished utterly.

The Greek's reverence for the impenetrable mystery of Egypt was profound. Light-hearted and volatile as he was, he scarcely knew what to make of the solemn and mystic Egyptian, and stood in awe of him; though he might ridicule at home the peculiarities of degenerate Egyptian forms of worship. He was in living contact with the things of a civilization, older then than any with which we may come into intimate touch today. It was a life, further in age from his own, than any we can know. If the wonder of the great buildings impresses our civilization, so developed in mechanics, how must these buildings, in their perfection, have impressed the imagination of the early Greek! It was back of his beginning. Altho' it is further from us, we understand it better.

The Greek never read the Egyptian's heart, nor even perfectly his written records, and accepted his story second-hand.† Our age has gone back to read the earliest writings. Neither did the

*This is the period dealt with in Ebers' "Egyptian Princess."
†As we know by comparisons.

EVENING AND THE MORNING 191

Greek know the mysterious significance of the temple construction, yet he dreamed a truth behind the veil.

The Greeks found in the buildings, not only forms, but ideas, and added their own particular life genius to the interpretation.

As for the Egyptian religion, it not only influenced the other nations, but itself spread over the classic world. And out of Egypt came our most cherished belief, the belief in the life hereafter.

Backward past the Empire with its great capital of the god Amon; past the temple developments during the rich feudal conditions of the Middle Kingdom, the evening looked to the golden morning. The state god Amon had now declined in the far highlands of the Upper Nile. For when the new state of Egypt had become organized and was reaching out and making connections with the world in the North, the conservative, priestly state of Amon loosed its hold and drew together, withdrawing itself further up the Nile, and moving its capital beyond the Cataracts. Its written language ceased to be Egyptian and has never yet been deciphered by the world. There, far away, for a time, it continued to exist, gradually perishing of its isolation; while because it was mysterious and out of reach, the Greeks looked upon it as the source of all which they knew, perhaps considering truly that even as we must advance from the known to the unknown, so from the unknown must once have proceeded the known. In this last stronghold perished Amon. Thus ended the romance of the Ethiopian Kingdom.

Neither did Re survive; though the worship of this possibly Eastern god of Heliopolis had been so predominant, since the Fifth Dynasty were established as his sons, that all the kings were supposed to be his incarnation, and he was therefore combined with Amon at Thebes.

But the first gods of three thousand years before —Osiris, Isis and Horus—had lived always in the hearts of the people. As the Restoration went back to the beginning, it was Osiris, Isis and Horus, who alone were resurrected. Just as Egypt had summarized her whole past, and was ready to hand on her influence, they gave the form which she bestowed on the world's religious thought.

CHAPTER XII

A Message from the Holy Places

TO understand the deepest significance of Mizraim, to know all that is meant by that occult saying, "Out of Egypt have I called my son," to realize what is symbolized by Jesus going down into Egypt and coming out from thence, we must visit the most holy place in the land. It is Abydos, the first sacred city, the Egyptian city of the holy sepulchre, the place of pilgrimage for more than three thousand years of human history. A fitting preparation is our own pilgrimage thither, the longest and most difficult of all our journeys in this most ancient land. Abydos is farther from the highway of the river than any other spot which we attempt to see. From Thebes we must go back a short way down the Nile. We leave by train at dawn to reach the nearest railway station and the donkeys. We return by train at midnight. One day!—one day in the Beginning, the First Day!

The temple at Abydos is the great Temple of Osiris, and is built upon the site of several earlier ones. Osiris is now supposed to be the earliest god of prehistoric Egypt, a god in human form, who with his story, had a mysterious apparent connection with a possibly earlier god, of a port on the Persian Sea. Osiris was the first and the last in the hearts of the people. His worship was the triumph of a popular belief, and, as we shall see, the Truth behind this earliest known religion, still persists.

This is the myth concerning him.

Osiris was an early and civilizing king of Egypt, who was treacherously slain by his brother Set. Isis, the wife of Osiris, found the body, which was then torn to pieces by Set; but Isis buried the pieces in fourteen places, which we know in history as the centres of the ancient nomes. The head was buried in Abydos, which thus became the most sacred spot. But afterwards Isis, by divine power, restored and revivified Osiris. He could no longer reign as an earthly king, but went to be the judge and ruler of the kingdom of the blessed. As that kingdom was in the West, he was called, "The first of those in the West," "the King of the glorified." And they said of every man, "As Osiris lives, so shall he also live." "They depart not as those who are dead but they depart as those who are living."*

Isis, remaining upon earth, gave birth to a son, Horus, whom she reared as the destroyer of Set and of the false slurs which Set cast upon Osiris. Thus the special mission of Horus in Egyptian mythology, is to take captive the power of darkness.

*Breasted's translation.

This story was probably shaped by actual events.

We have seen how, in historic days in Egypt, when a locality triumphs over the rest of the country and becomes its capital, and also when conquest is carried into other countries, the victory is always supposed to be the triumph of the god of the capital, who becomes for the time the supreme state god. Thus is history told in mythology. In view of such historic explanations of later stories, we may assume from the myth of Osiris and from statements made on temple walls,—as well as from recent revelations of prehistoric customs, especially with reference to the sacrifice of the king—that the prehistoric course of events was somewhat in the following order:

Osiris was the first god of Egypt, worshipped in the Delta and in Upper Egypt. He was probably that king whose civilizing mission was to introduce cultivation into the Nile Valley some 8,000 B. C. In the story of his sacrifice he sums up the fate of all the kings who had a reign of thirty years. Becoming a god in tradition, his worship was the monotheism of a tribe. This type of religion is always found preceding polytheism, which results when tribes unite and neither will give up its god. Fourteen centres of Osiris worship are known to have existed in prehistoric times, corresponding to the centres of the fourteen nomes into which Egypt was divided in the earliest dynastic days.

But there are traces of a very early Asiatic, and

probably Semitic, invasion of the Delta. It is even indicated that in days near to the most remote there was a Semitic principate in Heliopolis. These were the worshippers of Set, and it was they who killed Osiris in the story. Then a Delta tribe of Libyans, akin to the Osirians, and worshipping as their tribal goddess, the Virgin Isis, joined with the kindred race to conquer Set and reinstate Osiris. So, for a time all went well. However, a general swift decadence, found in the art of those darkest days just before history dawns, indicates a cataclysm. The Asiatics had probably returned in force and this was the scattering of Osiris' body. This time a tribe came from the south, another Libyan tribe, the worshippers of Horus.

Assuming leadership, they drove the followers of Set northward until they had forced them down the Red Sea.

Out of this shadowy development was personified the beautiful story, expressing all deepest human feelings, telling not only history, but the truths which underly all history.

The three great gods are blended in one story, a religion of the people, to touch the hearts of the self-conscious world for all time; for at this moment history dawns, the dark curtain rolls up, and the first historic King steps into the light—Menes, coming from near Abydos, and uniting with a strong hand Upper and Lower Egypt. He is the first King of all Egypt, and the first personage of whom records have been kept.

From this day forth, Abydos is holy ground, in which it was the desire of all the great of Egypt to be buried. The first stone structure known is a tomb at Abydos. As time went on and dynasties changed, the kings buried elsewhere,—at Memphis in the Old Kingdom, or Thebes in the Empire,—and their nobles were with them in the Old Kingdom. But the bodies were sent to lie on the holy ground for a time at least, or tablets were set up commending the dead to Osiris. Those whose missions north or south took them through this city, were able to use the occasion to satisfy their own most important personal desire by setting up a tablet for themselves, on which they generally recorded the chief events of their lives, and the mission which brought them to Abydos. Thus Abydos became a hoard of historical records and details, such as has been opened nowhere else in Egypt. Its burials, too, indicate the changes in the state; for, in the Sixth Dynasty, the nobles, instead of being buried around their ruler, are interred away from him, in Abydos. This indicates that the Old Kingdom was going to its decay. In the Middle Kingdom, in the case of a governor of a nome, he was buried in his nome, after being carried to Abydos.

In the tribal monotheism of the beginning, a god was not thought of as universal, nor was there any idea of objection to his affiliation with other tribal patrons. When, in the Middle Kingdom, out of the confusion of many gods, headed by the state god Re of Heliopolis,—a confusion which had gradually come upon Egypt through the jealousies of local priesthoods,—there developed the intuitive recognition of one power, to which the priests of each locality ascribed the attributes of their god, also ascribing to him universal attributes,—then Osiris, emerged supreme and it was the first movement in history toward a monotheism which should include the known world.

This was a prosperous age for Egypt. A new temple was built at Abydos. The priests put into dramatic form the story of Osiris; and annually, at a great festival, enacted it for the people, allowing them to take some share. Here then, at Abydos, some 2,000 B. C., was given the first drama of history, similar in intention to the mystic plays of the modern Middle Ages, and the Oberammergau play of today.

But the most remarkable phase of the religion of the triad, Osiris, Isis and Horus, was the inner development, the ethical standard which grew up in connection with it. The Egyptians, the first nation of history, made greater preparation for the future life than any other people has ever done. And in the very dawn of their history, they perceived that the future life must depend upon the purity of this. At first, as in the case of the Hebrews later, this was merely a ceremonial symbolic purity; but, by the Middle Kingdom and the triumph of Osiris, the heart of the people had spoken in a conscious and exalted ethical standard.

It was the ethical character of the life here which made the life hereafter. The justification of Osiris by Horus was the expression of their intuitive perception of the justification of the righteous. The heart was weighed in the balance with Truth and was light as the Feather of Truth if it knew no sin. This was probably a thousand years before such an ethical idea arose in Babylon or Israel.

Out of the supremacy of this one god, out of this ethical standard, developed an advanced conception of benevolence, which,—since it is the high impulse of the Universal working toward unity—we perceive as the most advanced and impersonal form of love. The inscriptions in the tombs of this time, such as that of Ameni at Beni-Hassan, while they may be exaggerated in their particular application, express the ideal of the period.

Such words as these we find:

"I gave bread to the hungry, water to the thirsty, clothing to the naked, and a boat to him who had none." "I was father to the orphan, husband to the widow, and a shelter to the shelterless."*

But the test was hard. With this high development went a danger. The priesthood, for worldly power and gain, developed a corresponding evil. The answers for the soul, which should carry it through the judgment were written out, leaving only the name to be inserted, and were sold, thus

*Breasted.

insuring the hereafter beforehand. It is this which has given us the Book of the Dead; and it is this which, in its denial of sins, has provided us with a full statement of the standard of the age. Heart scarabs were also sold, to lie upon a man's heart and prevent it from rising up to testify against him.

After the dark days of the disintegration of the Middle Kingdom and of the Hyksos invasion, when Thebes had again conquered Egypt, and the Empire was born, the worship of Amon-Re, and of the other members of the Amon triad, became the state religion; courage and conquest, rather than benevolence, became the ideal. Yet Thutmose I, conqueror and Emperor, while making glorious the Temple of Amon at Thebes, also restored the Temple of Osiris at Abydos, with great splendor and a special endowment for the offering of oblations. In his old age he turned toward Osiris in the sacred place of Abydos and there desired the perpetuation of his name and memory.

We have seen how, after Ikhnaton's break with the conventions, and the near approach of the state to an abstract conception in the worship of the Aton, Seti I, of the Nineteenth Dynasty, carried on the reorganization of the Empire, which restored the state gods. He built on the state temple to Amon. Yet he also turned his attention to Abydos, and erected there a temple to Osiris, and to the Osirian triad, as well as to the other great gods of Egypt. This seven-shrined temple,

OUR VILLA, THE SALEMLIK OF AN EASTERN PALACE

though much ruined, is in its carvings the finest example of the art of Egypt. Some influence of the freedom of the revolutionary school remains, with the spirit of the Nineteenth Dynasty. In Abydos, the strong, free drawing, similar to that of Seti's Karnak reliefs, is veiled in the most delicate modelling, such as we find in the Eighteenth Dynasty art; thus combining strength with feeling and refinement in a monument of rare charm and power.

Seti also built chapels for the services of the kings, dead two thousand years and buried here; and a list of the past Pharaohs which he placed on a wall, outlines Egyptian history for us today.

In order to endow this temple, Seti was obliged to open an unused route to certain mines back of Edfu, and journeyed himself two days into the desert to find water that the caravans might live.

Seti, however, did not finish this beautiful temple of Abydos. He died before he could complete it, or the great hall in Karnak, or his mortuary temple and university, now called "Kurna" at Thebes. He was buried in that tomb we entered, the reliefs of which are only second to those on the walls of this Temple of Abydos. It was left for the son, Rameses the Great, the herculean builder of Egypt, in whom her glory culminated, to finish not only the great hall of Karnak, the mortuary temple of Kurna, and the cliff temple at Abu Simbel, but the finest of all these, at Abydos, the most holy place, the place from near which came the first king of

Egypt, and where that first king is buried. Rameses undertook this work early in his reign, but left in Abydos the longest record of himself, with those poetic, filial statements in reference to Seti:

"It was his son who made his name live."
"Thou shalt be as if thou livest while I reign."*

But, as we now understand, the great formist, the vastness of whose building projects has never been equalled, the great maker of stone temples to the gods, of whom he felt himself to be one, became of necessity the Oppressor. Therefore, this rare temple of Abydos bespeaks also the outgoing of the Hebrews to receive their message and to give it to the world.

But there is a deeper, more mysterious building here, a secret, subterranean temple, with its hidden entrance in the temple of Seti I. It is in process of excavation today, because with the final raising of the great barrage at Assouan, its foundations will be flooded. We call it the Osireion, and it is unique in Egypt, for it is the secret place where was hoarded by the Pharaoh of the Exodus the hidden wisdom of Egypt. It tells of the life and death and resurrection of Osiris, it symbolizes the passage of the soul after death, and it is dedicated to the "Judge of the Dead."

From the beginning until the end of Egypt, Abydos was sacred. Who can visit it today and

*Breast's "Records of Ancient Egypt."

stand before the broken, beautiful temple—like that of the Ramesesum, most spiritual in its destruction,—who can see those tombs of all the ages, who can think over the story of Osiris, and not be stirred to the depths by the suggestion of things which have ever been, things which will ever be!

CHAPTER XIII

The Haunt of Horus

BUT the story is not complete, though we have found in Abydos, suggestions of religious and ritualistic forms which are strangely like a prophecy, and there has dawned upon us a knowledge that here are things which we recognize, so that we have looked with awe upon this once sacred city of the world.

Yet we must journey still further up the river, above Thebes; where the sandstone foundation of the Nubian desert gives way to the softer limestone of the desert of Egypt, and the river comes forth, unhindered on its way. Here, about seventy miles below the First Cataract, is the town of Edfu; and here, for much of the time until the great Twelfth Dynasty in the Middle Kingdom, was the boundary between Egypt and Nubia. Here, also, though there were several other centres, is the ancient stronghold of the worship of Horus, whence his religion spread to the north, when the worshippers of Horus conquered Set, and by uniting with the Osirians "justified Osiris."

There is a fragment of a list of kings, written in the Fifth Dynasty, just after the Pyramids were built, when men were already beginning to talk of the good days of old, and when they made the earliest attempt we know to put together a chronological record*. On the broken stone are a few prehistoric names, then already nearly a millenium old. They form the middle of a line, cut off in beginning and end, and without any facts in connection with them. These prehistoric kings are known to historic ages, only as the "Worshippers of Horus," and they slowly take on in the minds of the people a semi-divinity; becoming in tradition the half-gods.

They had followed the gods, who at first ruled Egypt,—Egypt, which was the world. Because the people of the first dynasties still remembered them as dead kings, they became the Divine Dead, or "the Dead," as they are spoken of in the history of Manetho, the Greek priest in the latter days of Egypt; and they are worshipped in their former capitals.

This association of divinity with kings was also a fact of all Egyptian history; due both to a story of incarnation, which became established as a conventional theory for every king of Egypt; and to the belief that the king's soul after death, partakes of the nature of Osiris, becomes Osiris. By the Eighteenth Dynasty this was said of every justified soul. The kings, therefore, provided temples for the worship of themselves.

When Menes,—in Egyptian tradition, as in the

*The so-called Palermo stone.

records, the first human king,—comes forward uniting the land, which had already become organized about the two centres of the North and the South, it is with the title of "Horus," for was he not the successor of the great god, who had also once ruled the whole of Egypt? Horus had come from the South to drive Set from the land, to vindicate and establish the goodness of Osiris, whose kingdom was now of the future world, and to reign on earth in his stead. Wherefore "Horus" is the symbol of royalty of this line who came from the South. The sign was the Horus hawk above the official name. Later, the Horus hawk trampling upon the sign of Set, was also shown. Psamtik, the Libyan, with the title of "Horus", for the last time drove Set from the land.

Horus, the beginning of whose worship may even be contemporaneous with the beginning of that of Osiris, went through probably a more confused history, with more varied aspects, more combinations, and thus more modifications than any god of Egypt. This is even developed to two Horuses, like the two Isoldes of the European legend. The sign-word "Horus", indicates "sky", and it is possible that two separate sky-gods have become confused by the similarity of name. The elder, as combined in the story, belonged to Letopolis, and was supposed to be a brother to Osiris. At Edfu, the younger becomes the elder Horus' son. The present temple of Edfu is dedicated to these two, and to the wife and mother, Hathor, who was combined with Isis. But the original Horus of Edfu and of Hieraconpolis, his other important centre, was an independent sky-god, symbolized by the hawk, which was ever the most sacred bird of Egypt. The souls of the kings were supposed to fly away as hawks, another possible connection of the kingship with this hawk-worshipping country where it originated. On the boat of Seker, god of the dead, who is represented by a mummified hawk, are many small hawks which represent the souls of the kings.

It is the hawk-god of Edfu whose place, as the conqueror of Set in the Osiris myth, though he was originally self-existent, is so strongly established that it proves the southern people to have been the conquerors of the Set worshippers or tribe. As connected with this triumph he is represented with a human body, and a hawk head. Upon the walls of his temple at Edfu, that victory is actually stated to have been a tribal conquest, which is an interesting point in connection with this building, the tradition of the priests confirming our belief that the old myth tells a prehistoric story.

Horus, the hawk, the sky-god, is the sun-god also. That Winged Sun we know so well above the temple gates is the symbol of Horus of Edfu. Throughout milleniums of Egyptian history, the sun, as the dominant influence on Egyptian physical life, was the dominant influence in Egyptian religion, especially in the practical and political affairs of this world. The worship of the sun-god in some form was always the state religion, and the history of Egypt was a religious history. While the first two strong dynasties from Thinis, near Abydos, held their sway, it was as the "Worshippers of Horus." With the rise to power of a Memphite family this worship waned, and by the close of the great Fourth Dynasty and the coming in of the Fifth, Re of Heliopolis had succeeded Horus, as the state god.

If there were, as seems probable, a predynastic Semitic principate at Heliopolis, the rise of Re in the Fifth Dynasty would mean that even this god, so characteristic of Egypt, came from the East, and that his coming was a return of Eastern influence.

It is impossible perfectly to extricate the gods, but at the time of Rameses, Re, as Amon-Re, was chief, and the theory of the after-life connected with him included all others. It was the idea of a long journey. At first Re might be the boatman to take the soul across to Osiris' Island of the Blessed, for that God of the Dead and the members of his triad, as well as all the other gods, were existing contemporaneously. But in Rameses' time the field of Osiris had become but one stage in the journey, when the soul accompanied Re through the watches of the night.

One of the symbols of Re was the Winged Sun, and the connection of Horus with Re is shown by the solar disk placed upon the head of the hawk, or upon the hawk-headed man, one of the most frequent combinations in Egypt.

The character of Horus as the sun-god coincides with his mission in the Osirian myth, to conquer darkness. His connection with Re is naively explained in a special story. The importance of the name to Egyptian minds has been mentioned. It was to the Egyptians the idea of the thing, without which it could not exist; and the knowledge of which, therefore, gave power over him who answered to it. Isis, by a clever stratagem, discovered the name of Re and thus obtained his two eyes, the sun and the moon, for her child. He becomes Hor-merti, "Horus of the two eyes," and the sacred eye of Horus becomes the principal amulet of Egypt.

By the dynasty of Rameses, Horus begins to assume an entirely human form. It is especially as the son of Isis, the holy child, that he appears from this time on. In an early and favorite representation, common down to Greek days, the boy is shown standing upon crocodiles,* holding poisonous reptiles harmless in his clasp. In Ptolemaic times he appears on an open lotus flower. But the baby, the loved, holy infant, alone or in his mother's lap, was the form which gradually took precedence of all others.

The splendor of Re had faded into night. In the latter days of Egypt, when the world was old, and the priests, those conservers of learning,

*There is a beautiful example in the Louvre.

were delving into ancient lore for a pure religion, hoping a renaissance, they tried to revive the worship of Amon-Re. But the only worship which had life in it was that earliest worship of the Osirian triad, and this now became the sole important cult in Egypt and spread out from there. Horus had again triumphed. For, not Amon-Re, but the holy infant, or the boy, became the most frequent figure on the temple walls and in the people's homes.

This, then is the story of him whose dwelling we are to see to-day. As the steamer makes its devious way up river, we descry above the palm-trees on the west, the great pylons, first as two huge, gray rocks, then as the towers of a fortress. The temple faces due south, and rises dominant over the little town of Edfy, as a mediaeval cathedral above a mediaeval city. It has been excavated from the mud of sun-dried brick habitations, clinging over and around it, and it stands revealed as the most perfect temple remaining in Egypt— quite perfect, though a little mosque in the town below is falling to decay. A thousand years younger than that seven-shrined temple at Abydos, this temple of Edfu was only one hundred and fifty years in building. But the priests of the Ptolemies' time, who superintended its construction, claim that it is built on the same plan as an old one on this site, which was erected by that Imhotep, of whom we hear so much, the great wise man and architect of King Zoser, who also built the Step-Pyramid.

THE HAUNT OF HORUS

With slight variations it is the same old temple plan,, *the* temple plan, which we found first in Dendera. Here the forecourt and pylons are complete. A girdle wall, built last outside of all, runs back from the court, securely enclosing the temple proper. It was always planned so— the whole temple facing and centered upon the within, and wall after wall outside, making the inner ever more inmost. Upon the walls of Edfu the Victories have passed away, for the Ptolemies did not record their conquests as the Pharaohs did. There is only an endless succession of gods and offerings. Except for some ancient geography, and the statement that the war between Horus and Set was a tribal war, little of interest is found written here. We enter between the pylons, to the great open court where the people thronged about the altar. In the eastern tower is a door which leads to a stairway, lighted by windows high in the walls, and there we mount to the height of 120 feet to overlook the temple. There are but two breaks in the roof beyond the court; one where a stone or two has fallen into the hypostyle hall; the other, a square opening above the sanctuary. Behind the hall, the roof is considerably lower and surrounded by a parapet. Over it, now so bare in the sunshine, once stretched a bright awning, making a cool and airy place above the heavy building. Like all the temples, this once rose aglow with gorgeous colors, in the midst of its green palms.

The people offered as best they knew, the best to the most holy,—as some men do to-day,—gold and silver and precious stones. The temple conserved their wealth.

It is all gone now. The walls are gray and empty. Outside, where the gardens bloomed, are the bare mounds of mud. And all lies silent forever, save when a horde of tourists swarms upon it. The temple is indeed a tomb, but with still a tomb's suggestion of the Life.

We go down from the tower to cross the sunny court, and pass through the hall of columns and through the vestibules. From each side of one of these, the corridor goes round the sanctuary, but we cross it to stand upon the threshold of that holy of holies, where only the holiest in the land, the king and the high-priest, might enter once a year. How the priests guarded it, even from the contamination of their own feet! Strangely enough, this inner place of mystery is now the lightest spot within the temple. That square hole in the roof above it appears almost as by intention; and the sun's rays stream into the farthest corner upon the shorn and empty shrine.

We are a small party, lingering for the quiet to think, and we realize how the Hebrews,—chosen, as they undoubtedly were,—were called to come out from the forms with which Egypt began and into which she had crystallized, and to take the next step, conserving the true Life. They kept the temple, leaving out the image from its sacred heart.

But here there is only the shell of something that once was brilliant. Walls upon walls of gray, empty and imageless now. Is no holiness in the ancient place that our feet stand here in the heart of silence? Yea, for here as elsewhere, it is in our own hearts we may find the holy stillness.

CHAPTER XIV

The Gift of Egypt.

WE have not yet reached the final destination of our pilgrimage. We shall find it at the First Cataract. So we return once more to the modern life on the steamer, and proceed as far as our boat can navigate, arriving at the Port of Assouan, a mud flat beside the town. We have passed from end to end of the land of Egypt. This is the farthest place in the earliest country. It is true that when Egyptian Civilization rose to the high tide of Empire and even at periods before, it overflowed the high lands of Nubia. But here was the natural and the established political boundary between the southern part of Egypt, and the sometime unorganized world beyond. Here, at the foot of the Cataract, was the ancient "Suan," or trade-market for the whole of the southland.

In this narrow valley that we have traversed for 750 miles from the coast, the Nile has cut its canon, nearly a thousand feet below the general level of the vast desert plateau, that most ancient highland to be raised above the water, stretching across Northern Africa and Central Asia;

THE GIFT OF EGYPT

has spread rich soil for the green crops on the floor of the canon; and provided, not only life, but a means of communication to bind together the people on its banks. In this cradle was the Beginning, with the breath of the pure desert in it; secured by the desert's walls and a further line of the desert mountains on the east, which guard it against invasion, even by clouds; protected on the northern end by the smooth coast of the seven-mouthed Delta, having no harbors; and on the south by this rocky barrier to navigation. Standing out alone in the desert, protected by it until they were strong enough to come forth and to wage combat—thus arose and looked about them the men of the first nation, with their early government,—a nation apparently alone in the desert of the world.

It is this protection in the narrow valley, with the gates at the north and the south, which, forbidding any sudden great invasion, has preserved the Egyptian type.

The geography of Egyptian children must have been simple. In this unique country, to "go up" was to leave the snug valley, "to descend" was to come home. The first idea of north was "downstream," and when the Egyptians had crossed the desert, and discovered the Euphrates, they called it the "inverted water," for they were accustomed to going upstream to the south. Here at this First Cataract, the large palm-covered island of Elephantine, which leads the van of granite elevations that trouble the waters and seem tumbling down the river—was known as the "Door of the South."

It was the seat of adventurous nobles, who often fared forth with their troops into darkest Africa. Their tombs are in the cliffs on the western shore of the river. On the eastern bank is Assouan, the ancient "Suan," now for Europeans, the health-resort par excellence in Egypt. The winds which blow over it still pass over hundreds of miles of clean, pure desert, unpolluted by organic life. On the island of Elephantine is a luxurious modern European hotel with its gardens; on the shore opposite, a line of modern houses, shutting out of sight the cramped village of the modern natives. A little further upstream, in a small bay of the river, is another luxurious hotel establishment.

In our search for the things of the Past, we are still interested by the way. Assouan bears the mark of a border town, a trading-market between different regions. Today the river street of the place gives us a greater variety of living interest than almost any street in Egypt. Between the trees which border it, we look down upon a mud flat or beach below, while the little boats, the bright colored feluccas of the natives, under sail and oars, ply back and forth between the shore and Elephantine. On the street itself we are overwhelmed by donkeys and camels with importunate drivers. The donkeys and the boys seem quite familiar; but the camels are taller than those we know,

THE GIFT OF EGYPT 217

and are white except where decorated with henna. They appear more than ordinarily ill-natured; and after watching one askance, as he performed a sort of spinning dance, in the middle of the road, endeavoring to rid himself of a rider, we decided to hold our ambitions in check. The owners of these animals are the Bicharines, whose camp outside of Assouan is one of the sights of the locality. It is a large group of huts, made of mats; and in front of each primitive dwelling are children playing and one of these white camels,— with a leg tied up to prevent his running away. The Bicharines are totally unlike the Egyptians, blacker, and always dressed in white; their distinguishing characteristics are their mops of hair and their pride. Sometimes the hair of girls is done in a hundred braids, standing out like flame. They are all tall and straight as American Indians, and perhaps would bear civilization as ill. Yet there seems a native nobility, something fine about such natures, something freer than could be found in any civilization.

We, ourselves, experience a small instance of their pride. Tourists have been requested in notices posted everywhere by the government, not to give bakshish, since it spoils industry and pauperizes the natives. Before going up the Nile, we made enquiries of photographers as to the proper amount to give for posing; and from a grocery-shop supplied ourselves with the small coins in use among the natives. One day, as we are passsing through the streets of Assouan, three Bicharine boys, catching sight of the camera, as children always do, instantly fling themselves into position for a picture. It is over in a second, and several coins given to each boy. But they have been accustomed to fees, which equal the price of a day's work in excavating; and the leader, like a little lord, marches up magnificently and lays his coins in my friend's hand. The others, not to be outdone, follow suit. "Very well," says my friend, "Thank you for the picture." If they are taken aback, they make no sign, but proudly walk away.

Back of the river street of Assouan, in the native town, are fascinating native bazaars, small, open shops, indicating greater poverty and simplicity than those of Cairo. Their wares are largely Nubian and Sudanese, of less value, and yet for that very reason more rare, than the Egyptian scarves and jewelry, imported over Europe. We remember the old trade-routes into Nubia for ivory and treasure, and how once the control of them all was put with great ceremony into the hands of one man, who was called the "Keeper of the Door of the South"*

There is much of very ancient interest about Assouan. Here ancient astronomers observed in a well that the sun at this point cast no shadow at noon; and used the knowledge as a basis for correct earth-measurements. Over on Elephantine is an old Nilometer, which still marks the rise and

*Breasted.

THE GIFT OF EGYPT

fall of the river. Near to Assouan are the granite quarries, which fill us with awe as the place whence so many wondrous forms came forth, associated with all the jubilees of the Pharaohs of Egypt. Particularly was the granite cut for the thirty year jubilee, so imposingly celebrated in the Eighteenth Dynasty, but apparently a development of the thirty year jubilee and sacrifice of the king in prehistoric times, out of which came the details of the burial of Osiris.

In the time of the Empire, every jubilee was the occasion for an expedition under a competent officer to secure granite obelisks from these quarries. One such block, whose story is unknown, still lies by the old road.

Such an expedition to the border was an affair of peace, as was the trade with the Southland, but the portal whence this trade came in was the "Door" through which all the expeditions of conquest in the south went out, re-entering victorious. And the records of all these various kinds of missions, from the earliest days until the end, were written by king and commander, a lasting memorial, on the rocks in the midst of the river.

Yet the interest of all these things grows pale in the significance of one. Here is not only the anciently supposed source of the inundation and a present source of health, but a shrine of something deeper. Five miles from Assouan, at the upper end of the islands which made the Cataract, is an island gem which holds the secret,—Philae, the pearl of Egypt, "the most beautiful and the most historic little island in the world."

The great dam is between us and Philae—and already this island is vanishing. We may plan our journey to it in various ways. The most interesting method, if it be desired to crowd all into one day's travelling, is to go by donkeys past the old quarries to "Shellal,"—the Arab name for Cataract—an Arab town, which is opposite to Philae; and taking a felucca there and back, to return on the donkeys by way of the great barrage. But the donkey-boys of Assouan appear quarrelsome and disorderly to us; there is no Aboudi, and we left our friends at Luxor when we came on this pilgrimage. So we set out by train for Shellal, on the small branch road, which carries goods past the Cataract and dam. Having dispensed with the troublesome offices of a dragoman, we nearly fall into the hands of the vociferous felucca rowers at Shellal. We do not go to the Holy Isle in the barque of the sun-god Re. Most fortunately for us, we come upon a little company of old friends from America, who take us in with them.

But,—where is Philae, the remote little island, famous to the ends of the earth? Here and there above the river wave the heads of slender palm trees. They are up to their necks in water, and we wend our picturesque way among them. Then we come upon a graceful little building, like and yet unlike the pictures with which we have been familiar since childhood—the small kiosk, called

WATER-JARS

by the natives, "Pharaoh's Bed." It was unfinished. Was it perhaps intended for a temple after that very perfect style, the cella temple, brought in under Amenhotep III? Even if so, today it is empty of a sanctuary and looks up to the open sky. There are only, upon a small rectangular wall, the graceful columns, each capital different from all the rest. Terraced walls have held the earth in a firm base below it, groups of palm trees cluster lovingly about it. But there is no island visible today, nothing but tufted bits of unusual heights, and the waving crests of the palms. Our felucca glides on and we find ourselves within the enchanted enclosure, the empty rectangle of pillars set against the blue of water and sky. Before we have more than caught the vision, we have passed through it, out upon the expanse of waters over the site of the sacred isle.

Going southward, we appear before the entrance to the temple of the island. Since earliest times this place is supposed to have been sacred to Isis. It is the Temple of Isis that we have come to see. Not so large not yet so perfect as the Temple of Horus at Edfu, and built at as late a day, this temple is still unfinished, but its exquisite surroundings and the fresh coloring within its chambers have long given modern travellers the most comprehensive impression of a temple in its living beauty—when Egypt was Egyptian. The life seems not wholly gone. And now the waters have crept up softly, almost stealthily, and have flowed into it.

The temple plan was slightly modified to suit the contour of the island. The forecourt before the first pylon, is almost a triangle. Our little boat, a bright note of color, enters at the narrower end, and we float between the colonnades, almost beside the capitals. Behind the long line to our left is the river wall. We pass through the first pylon, where the rowers pause on their oars, that we may see in the gateway the tablet which commemorates Napoleon's visit to the island. A small door in the face of the left pylon tower leads into the birth chapel, which forms one side of the inner court. Across this second court, we reach the second pylon, set at a slightly different angle to the first. The doorway leads into the hypostyle hall, and thus to the holy of holies, with its chambers beyond. Even here the water has slipped over the floor and now forbids us; the rich, soft, beautiful colors of the flower capitals are reflected by it, as we look within from our boat. This reflective water, like a self-consciousness is significant, and perfects while it destroys the temple.

In the pylon tower at our left is a narrow passage, where a loose board-walk permits our stepping over to the stair, and so we ascend to the roof, or, climbing further, to the top of the pylon. We two slip away to visit the little chapel of Osiris, tucked in a corner of the roof, and open to the sky. We descend a few steps to examine the exquisite reliefs which tell the story, probably the oldest story known. Afterward, from the pylon, we look over the waters:—southward into Nubia; east to Shellal, beyond the little kiosk; close on our west to Bigeh, an island once also consecrated; and far to the north, where we descry a long, cold line of masonry. There is the evidence that it is modern mechanics which has laid a cold hand on the sacred little island, to destroy it.

But the secret of Philae is already possessed.

Leaving the soft light from the firmaments above and below us, and descending the narrow, dark stairway in the temple, we re-embark in our gay little boat, with its swarthy Egyptian rowers, and again float out upon the waters, looking backward all the way. And first the reflections, the colors, and the shadows of the dim hypostyle hall with the chambers behind and beyond it, are lost to view, leaving the doorway dark —for it is open. The dark doorways, one behind another, always suggest a mystery. We are alone with the temple, and the ripples from our oars seem to caress the walls and columns. Across the court, past the birth chapel, we move, and through the outer doorway, gain the outer court, whose colonnades seem all but to meet before us. But we glide between the long lines and out at the entrance. The temple is behind us.

The felucca turns north along the temple wall, passing between Bigeh and Philae. Palm-trees, rocks, desert cliffs and water make a picture of unconquered and forbidding Nature. But as Philae is lost to us, we come into view of the great barrage. It is the stone wall against which the waters of the Past have beat in vain, for it hoards, the material water by means of which the life of the Present takes form.

It is a vast lake which the great dam keeps back. When we reach the line of masonry, we can go no further, and leaving our boat, climb by steps up the wall. Here small hand trolleys await us, the seats like those in a trap, back to back. We are trundled merrily along the top of the wall for over a mile; near us on one side, the sight of the water; below us on the other, the sound of a hundred falls. Now and then we are permitted to alight and look over the parapet, where the water gushes out through the openings which are all arranged at different heights to break the strain, and are regulated by gates.

At the further end, are the house of the engineer and a smaller building, where, once more, the ubiquitous Cook provides for the wayfaring man. But we have our lunch with us; and another felucca waits below to take us through the lock. Again we sail forth. Our twelve happy-natured rowers, one a child with a child's enthusiasm over helping, chant weirdly with the rhythm of the oars. As their clear-cut faces swing back, we are grotesquely reminded of their forefathers in the Cairo Museum. When the boat is at rest in the dock, they give up to their singing, beating upon

THE GIFT OF EGYPT

small drums made of gourds. To their religious chant, we lightly pass the place where a few years ago natives risked their lives to earn a living by the sport of shooting the Cataract on logs. They are at home in the water, these people. A small black boy swims out to us on a log, claiming piastres for doing it. Childhood is merry in Egypt. Child voices sing like birds over the hard labor of excavating. We wind our way among the rocks, which so unmoved, create such tumult. These are the rocks of records so full, that were all Egypt washed away, they might still tell a continuous story. They are strangely black above the water. We turn into a channel between two islands, and draw up to a small beach, which lies serenely basking towards the southern sun. This is the island of Sehel, and upon it is an inscription viewed with wonder and awe by students of Hebrew story.

The line of a crack drawn clear across the rock does not cancel its weather-beaten record of a seven year's famine in Egypt. The story relates how the river failed to rise for seven years and how the king summoned his wise man who advised a sacrifice to the Potter-god of the Cataract. The sacrifice was answered by the inundations, and the land of the Cataract was consecrated to Khnum. This was, perhaps, a thousand years before the time of Joseph, in the reign of that king Zoser, whose tomb is the Step-Pyramid, and who is reported to have built the first temple of Horus at Edfu. The record of the tradition was written much later by the priests of Khnum, in support of their claim to the region. But it shows that such famines were not unthinkable, indeed had occurred in Egyptian experience.

From the beach of Sehel we climb the venerable and broken rocks, above which waves the grass—and last year's seeds. They are blown with the sand. In a windswept corner of the shelf we spread our lunch. Chancing to look below, we see on the beach, beyond the empty boat, a line of mats on which twelve rowers kneel in prayer. It is their first moment of rest since the noon hour. Here away in the sight of the God of nature, such prayer seems not to resemble the self-conscious praying of the street corners. Religion is still the secret of Egypt.

As the sun moves westward we start once more, "If this were anywhere but Egypt, I should say it was going to rain," exclaims one of our party; and almost before the words are spoken—the rain comes. The rowers spring to the curtains; but sharply as it began, just so suddenly it is over, the one shower of three years, which will ever after serve to date our pilgrimage to Philae.

One more stop we make, this time at the old Nilometer on Elephantine, by the steps of which we climb to the green surface of the island. Here at the "border" of Egypt, in the time of Jeremiah and after, lived the Jewish colony, whose houses have just been excavated by French and German

THE GIFT OF EGYPT

expeditions. From Elephantine, we return, tired out, to modern tea at Assouan.

But our thoughts turn back to the temple, and what it signifies. They watch the creeping destruction of the water. Long before Moses was forced to look for water in the wilderness that was the task of the Egyptians, and has been, as we have seen, ever since. Their river furnishes an initial supply, but they must learn how to conserve it ere they can use it. This was their first practical problem and out of it practical mechanics was born in the dawn of human history. Working upon that same problem today, the engineers of one of the most advanced of modern nations, have constructed here, at the farthest place in the land of Egypt, the greatest barrage in the world.

It pays the interest on Egyptian bonds; it does a greater and more vital thing, it brings life to the people of the land of Egypt today. But the government and the engineers—do they know what they do in placing it here? Do they know what this beautiful temple, soon to be merely a mound of earth and stones, really is? The shrine of the idea of holy motherhood in the world!

Just before the Christian era dawned, this oldest story of all had gained its strongest hold upon the people, and that phase of it, the motherhood of Isis, was the phase most loved, most often represented, most dwelt upon,—the thought which was worshipped here. Isis and Horus, divine mother and child, lived in the hearts of the people, and so strong was this worship that it spread to Rome, and with Rome to all the conquests of the Roman Empire,—preparing a way. Then arose Christianity in Asia.

The supreme message of the Jews was brought to consciousness and fulfilled to the, world. The trust for which they were developed and cherished and chastened for centuries, was not for themselves alone, but in the fulness of time for the uplifting of humanity. When the Jews had given birth to this consciousness, their own protecting husks of formalism were destroyed by it. But it was back in Alexandria, that Christianity took strong root, and swept from end to end of Egypt, and out into the world. No teacher has ever presented such an ethical standard as Jesus. Yet it was in Egypt, not in the old state religion of Re or Amon-Re, but in the earliest religion of the people,—the story of Isis, Horus and Osiris,—that the form was established. Egypt, always crystallizing forms, did so, above all, in the realm of ideas. Her gods had become concentrated, they were now transformed, as a dream changes to the reality which it still overshadows. Christianity came forth with all the elements of the Egyptian story, and developed similar accompanying ideas of monasticism, and of organized priesthoods and ritual.

The priesthoods of Egypt, especially those of Isis, had undoubtedly low forms of attracting the people; they had developed an unworthy side of

THE GIFT OF EGYPT

secret mysteries, and that great evil of perverting truth by forms of psychic magic. In Europe the worship of Isis, as Isis, came into strong combat with early Christianity.

But gradually the ideas of Christianity in Europe underwent a transformation.

In the religion of Egypt we find not only heaven and hell, but the monasticism, mysticism and dreamy abstractions of later Christianity, which undoubtedly came from this source and for the development of which we cannot credit the pure and simple precepts of Jesus. The life of Christendom as a whole has not rested in these forms—on the other hand, it has never yet reached the full depth of those simple, vital teachings, which reveal the inmost source of active life.

The Coptic Church, the Church of Egypt, and the oldest Christian Church still in existence, destroyed in Egypt the old temples, though the worship of Isis, enthroned in this remote island, continued as her worship until the Fifth century of the Christian era.

As in other nations, before there was thought of woman's inferiority, so in Egypt, "the classic home of woman's power," woman's counsel and decisions in affairs of state were supposed to be divine. Just as Egypt was about to pass on her message to the world, not only did the royal descent through mother and daughter, assume if possible, greater importance than ever, but the High Priesthood of Amon belonged to a woman and descended in the royal female line; while at the same time the worship of motherhood in Isis had become almost alone in its supremacy. Then Isis, earliest form of the eternally true ideal of a mystic Motherhood, purified from the evils attending her worship, rose into the Christian Madonna.

Breasted sees in the revival of Egypt and in the Osirian story, the preparation for doctrinal Christianity; Petrie says,"The Hebrews might give us the pure Virgin Mary, they could never have given us the glorified Madonna."

But let us understand the reason. Is it not because Egypt, the first nation of history, the beginning of the continuously developing material civilization of the West, stands therefore above all for Form, and so gives form to all that is to follow?

It was the idea enshrined here, of holy Motherhood, which, like a symbolic prophecy, prepared Egypt to receive Christianity, and which, transformed by Christianity, continues to influence the world. "Out of Egypt have I called my son," is an Eastern saying of deep, occult wisdom. As Egypt represents the material and objective reasoning which has been most strongly developed in the West and in the masculine nature, is not this idea of sonship the symbol subconsciously given, which represents the objective or Form, recognizing its source in the subjective or Life?

CHAPTER XV

Light

THE Sphinx of Egypt represents the kingdom of the material world. At the feet of the Sphinx we looked upon Form, the objective idea of God, as his outer material realm.

It sends us dreaming, back before the Past.

When the world was formed, and when the universe achieved, had risen to consciousness, Man stood there at the gate, beginning his long pilgrimage to God upon the outside. By objective knowledge, which for a time seems partly to separate him from the Creator, he goes back through God's whole expressed creation, the realm of symbols, the world of Form, in order that he may consciously know when at last, in that holy of holies, farthest within himself, he finds the God whom he has felt behind the veil.

With the first written word was thought given a limiting, conventional form. This earliest nation, while still full of subjective feeling, had to make the beginning of objective knowledge from the most outward plane; and to give the thought its outer form or symbol, that it might be conveyed from soul to soul by way of sense to sense. In the early myths of Egypt we find the importance of the Name, the word standing for the idea of the thing and thus representing its soul. In the days of the Empire there developed the belief in the Word, the expression of a definite thought, as the means of creation. It is similar to the later Greek doctrine of the "Logos," to the "God said" of the Hebrew Genesis, and the "Word" of the Greek-influenced addition to the Hebrew Scripture.

In the beginning was simple, graphic language with the heart in it; true poetry, dealing with the universal individual. But a written word is a reflection, making men conscious of their thought. Therefore was the beginning of writing the awakening of the soul's self-consciousness. Then was the Truth enshrined in a garden of symbols, even as the Spirit is enshrined in the temple of Man's body.

Every word is itself a symbol, as we can see in Egypt, where the process of creating signs for writing, is revealed in the records of centuries.

The nation could not have come into being until the creation of a system of writing was first achieved. The government could not otherwise have carried on any wide-spread administration. Egypt had developed not only syllables, but an alphabet of twenty-four letters, 2,500 years before any other people.* The office of the scribe became the most exalted in Egypt. Not yet overwhelmed with the making of many books, nor

*Breasted.

with the multiplicity and vanity of words, they cherished each written treasure, their wonder at its existence not yet passed away. Thus began objective history—one continuous growth, with a long period of preparation behind it. The flowering of our civilization has been, after all, so brief, from Egypt until now,—the shining of the consciousness of the race into self-consciousness.

Egypt, still subjective, was beginning with the outermost. Therefore her strange perversions, her strange combination of extremes, of intense religious feeling with the most conventional forms, wrought into stone temples such as the world has never seen—they are today most valuable for the writing on the walls. Translated into modern languages, Egypt's records now can never be lost. This early nation was the most conservative, holding fast to things both good and bad. The Truth was enshrined in symbols, and the symbols were cherished as the Truth.

We have read the story of the state religion, and how there went with it all the forms of a religious calendar, with its feast days, and an elaborate ritual; and how the state was under the control of the form of its religion, until the religious form absorbed the state. There were the soldiers, or conquering class; the priests, or conserving class; and the Third Estate, the workers, the body of the people. The priesthoods not only possessed enormous revenues, but endowments of land exempt from taxation, as did the bishoprics of the modern

Middle Ages. As the English king today is the head of the English Church, so was the Pharaoh the nominal head of the religion of Egypt.

But it is not only in the outer observances, nor in the word alone that we see the forms we know. We find such forms in the ideas themselves. Such symbols as the Potter, for God the Creator, which we may use, were actually pictured in Egypt; such an aspect of God was separately personified. We find also the deluge, the serpent of evil and the flames of hell, against which a ritual prayer was uttered by the priests of Karnak every morning. The idea of a divine Fatherhood, glimpsed in a distorted fashion and scarcely grasped as universal; the resurrection of Osiris; the Madonna idea in Egypt—were they not symbols arising from and predicting everlasting Truth? Is not Form the symbolic expression of Truth?

Does a knowledge of these matters disturb us by a change of thought which tempts us, not only to cast all these things away, since we find them what Moses himself once cast off, but with them what, in our own religion, they now suggest? Shall we, in our pride of knowledge, throw away the spiritual kernel because we think we know the intellectual husks? Shall we not rather see in these early symbols, at once a confirmation, and a suggestion that the Truth lies deeper than we have yet known? Not only are observances symbolic, but ideas themselves express the inner Truth.

In the light of our Christian era the form of our religion does appear to go back behind the Jews to that story which grew out of the earliest consciousness of mankind and which prepared the way, the story which was itself transformed by Christianity. The Christian religion of the Western world had its beginning, not in the East, from whence came its life, but in the earliest nation of history, the first nation of the West, the first of the material, masculine part of the world which has held the ideal of conquest and has worshipped womanhood. The exaltation of woman, which culminated in the idea of the glorified Madonna, was not, as some historians think, the weakness of Egypt. It was due to the fact that Egypt was West, was material, was masculine; and its purpose was deep as the foundation of humanity. The idea of the Madonna made Christianity acceptable and understandable to the young masculine civilization of Europe. The Egyptians looked ever to the West, as the land toward which they were to pass. They spoke of Osiris as "the first of those in the West". That they saw the West as the land of Death was itself symbolic, since it is the land of Form, while the East is the land of Spirit or Life.

But for us the wonder has grown with the realization that back in the time of Moses there was hidden away in the dark secret places on the westward side of Egypt, dreams which, though distorted, seem like prophecy; that these dreams waxed strangely strong above all others in the hearts of the people just before the light dawned in the East, and so Egypt, the earliest of nations, was prepared to welcome and establish Christianity and to pass it on with all her great influence to the Western world.

So we think of Egypt as the builder of the Temple, symbolized by the actual temple form which that nation gave to the world, the temple form which Israel later had. So also, Egypt stands for the image of each attribute of God, and for the preservation of the material body as the essential to immortality. All religion is the outer expression of man's inner consciousness of God. But the Egyptians, as we have seen, began their search for God upon the outside, piling up the stones in temples,—in which they imprisoned and corrupted their faith.

Moses took the next great step toward inner Truth when he led his Semitic people out of the land of Rameses, cast off the images, and gave them the Divine Law instead.

It remained for Jesus, the perfect culmination of his race, to reveal the Spirit behind the Law.

We can only know Truth as it is individualized in some personal experience, yet the Truth itself is not in those outer historical facts of experience or personality which may be disputed, it is within and universal.

The Story of Jesus, heralded milleniums before, and repeated in many religions, is a universal story, more deeply true than any facts of history, truer than any of the relative facts known in our octave of scientific perception.

Science, which belongs to the West, explains from the outside; as religion, from the inside. Science should be symbolic of religion, even as the material form is expressive of the inmost. And now science itself is literally unearthing these dreams which belong to the earliest records of Time; this prehistoric story which curtains a great Truth.

Has not the world at last reached that stage in the great rhythm of human consciousness, when it can go back to the images Moses cast off, and, separating them from perverted observances, read their real significance?

The West, the objective consciousness, is now the self-consciousness of the world. And one of the great interests of our age has been the exploration of this oldest, buried civilization, which, sealed away for thousands of years, shall achieve immortality through the lessons it gives to us.

Wonderful indeed that the first civilization should have grown up in this valley, that the earliest records might be given to this most perfect climate in the world for preservation; wonderful, that its people should have built more largely and strongly than any others, that they should have spent their existence to preserve the bodies of their dead and their "houses of eternity!" The speed of history is accelerated now, and we are hurrying Time with steam and electricity to catch each moment. And what will happen—now that we have unearthed the Past, and exposed it to destruction?

Is it not that all our return to the first stage of development from which we have become separated through change of material forms, must be a return to the spirit?

The treasures may not last another hundred years; and our age, which has learned to read, has, in unearthing, destroyed. But is it not because our age is ripe for spiritual understanding that Egypt, covered and preserved for centuries, has been revealed to us,—even though the revelation mean the destruction of Egypt?

We two think it over, on the pathless desert, while the Sands of Time sweep round us and the heavens open above the distant pyramids, for the golden afterglow.

Egypt is an atmosphere of translucent color in which we find the ruins of the Past—a partial material resurrection out of which develops the perfect resurrection of its significance.

Down by the river the women of Egypt, black-draped against the sunset, are drawing water. Beautifully developed figures, lithe and strong; brilliant eyes, and faces which have become strangely familiar, faces which are of the same form as those of thousands of years ago.

As we watch the simple picture of a girl carry-

LIGHT

ing water, the mystery which runs through all of Egypt is explained.

It is *Life* which the girl herself carries down through centuries of change and serfdom; Life,—even through Death,—of which the ancient Egyptians were so intensely conscious; which they worshipped in animals; worshipped more in their own conscious intelligence; for it was Life, in the first strong impetus of the Beginning; Life which they felt, with the early wisdom of revelation, *must* carry:—as it will, though through centuries of oblivion, of servitude and of degradation, until an enlightened West shall come to read deeper than words, the message of the Past, the message of Spiritual Immortality.

www.ingramcontent.com/pod-product-compliance
Lightning Source LLC
Chambersburg PA
CBHW050926240426
43670CB00022B/2941